D1006848

Worship is a subject that is difficult, sometimes painful, for many believers today. In *Heights of Delight*, Dick Eastman, a beloved and godly brother, shows us how worship is not only infinitely pleasing to God and vital to our spiritual growth but is absolutely necessary to bring the nations to a saving knowledge of our Lord and Savior Jesus Christ.

DR. BILL BRIGHT
FOUNDER AND CHAIRMAN
CAMPUS CRUSADE FOR CHRIST

For two decades I've experienced firsthand Dick Eastman's delight in Christ through intercessory worship (before anyone even called it that!). For hours and days we have prayed together over the years. As a result, I've discovered that when you combine Dick's passion for God, his intercessory soul and his seasoned ministry to the nations, you have an author who can transform any life, taking one to the heights. I know Dick has done it for me!
Let his newest book do it for you.

DAVID BRYANT
PRESIDENT, CONCERTS OF PRAYER
CHAIRMAN, AMERICA'S NATIONAL PRAYER COMMITTEE

I believe the insights from *Heights of Delight* will catalyze a fresh initiative of global worship, worship evangelism and worship anticipation among God's people worldwide that could well usher in the return of our Lord.

LUIS BUSH
CO-FOUNDER OF AD2000 & BEYOND MOVEMENT
PASADENA, CALIFORNIA

This is a timely book in this season of crisis. The need to weave these twin emphases—worship and intercession—has never been as strategic as it is now. God has always looked for two kinds of people: intercessors and worshipers. Dick Eastman masterfully blends these colors in his book *Heights of Delight* and does what few have done heretofore: demonstrates the symbiotic relationship of worship and intercession. In our communion with God, we must both inhale and exhale. Worship is the inhale, intercession the exhale. We need both, and Eastman has captured the rhythm of the two in a masterfully strategic way.

STEVE FRY
PRESIDENT, MESSENGER FELLOWSHIP, INC.
AUTHOR, *I AM THE UNVEILING OF GOD*

I've respected, admired and supported the work of Dick Eastman for years. He is faithful and steadfast and is a source of wisdom for missions-minded Christians everywhere. Once again, Dr. Eastman effectively reminds us that our most important task is the worship of God and that worship is intrinsically connected to fulfilling God's plan for humankind.

TED HAGGARD
PASTOR, NEW LIFE CHURCH
COLORADO SPRINGS, COLORADO

Dick Eastman's gift of an intercessor's passion for, and power in, partnership with God is multiplied over and over to us all by means of the understandable, practical, "believe-I-can-do-this" guidance and help he gives people like you and me. Under Jesus' touch, he teaches us to pray!

JACK W. HAYFORD, LITT.D.
CHANCELLOR
THE KING'S SEMINARY
VAN NUYS, CALIFORNIA

Heights of Delight is a book that will literally take you to new heights of understanding when it comes to worshiping Almighty God. I can think of few men who are better qualified than Dick Eastman to speak on the incredible value—and power—that praise and prayer hold in the Lord's economy. If we all worshiped like this, our churches, nations and world would be forever transformed.

BILL MCCARTNEY
FOUNDER AND PRESIDENT
PROMISE KEEPERS

My heart trembled with praise and joy as I read *Heights of Delight*. This book is a gracious gift to the Church and a feast for the hungry soul.

ADRIAN ROGERS
PASTOR, BELLEVUE BAPTIST CHURCH
MEMPHIS, TENNESSEE

I love it when the Holy Spirit breathes new life into an old truth. In this new book *Heights of Delight*, the Lord has shown Dick Eastman some powerful truths regarding endtime global harvest for the Body of Christ. God is still interested in one thing: souls! So let's not miss this new move of the Spirit. I believe with all my heart that intercessory worship is the key to bringing the manifest presence of God to the earth. He's coming *to* us before He comes *for* us!

RICKY SKAGGS
ENTERTAINER, NASHVILLE, TENNESSEE

HEIGHTS

of

DELIGHT

HEIGHTS

of

DELIGHT

DICK EASTMAN

Regal

From Gospel Light
Ventura, California, U.S.A.

Published by Regal Books
From Gospel Light
Ventura, California, U.S.A.
Printed in the U.S.A.

Regal Books is a ministry of Gospel Light, an evangelical
Christian publisher dedicated to serving the local church. We
believe God's vision for Gospel Light is to provide church leaders
with biblical, user-friendly materials that will help them evangelize, disciple and minister to children, youth and families.

It is our prayer that this Regal book will help you discover
biblical truth for your own life and help you meet the needs
of others. May God richly bless you.

*For a free catalog of resources from Regal Books/Gospel Light,
please call your Christian supplier or contact us at* 1-800-4-GOSPEL
or www.regalbooks.com.

Rights for publishing this book in other languages are contracted by
Gospel Light Worldwide, the international nonprofit ministry of
Gospel Light. Gospel Light Worldwide also provides publishing and
technical assistance to international publishers dedicated to producing
Sunday School and Vacation Bible School curricula and books in
the languages of the world. For additional information, visit
www.gospellightworldwide.org; write to Gospel Light Worldwide,
P.O. Box 3875, Ventura, CA 93006; or
send an e-mail to info@gospellightworldwide.org.

Cover design and Interior by Robert Williams
Edited by Benjamin Unseth

Library of Congress Cataloging-in-Publication Data
Eastman, Dick.
  Heights of delight / Dick Eastman
        p. cm.
Includes bibliographical references.
  ISBN 0-8307-2946-1
  1. Worship I. Title.
  BV10.3 .E27 2002
  248.3—dc21   2001007604

1 2 3 4 5 6 7 8 9 10 / 09 08 07 06 05 04 03 02

DEDICATION

To Bill:
Thanks for launching me
on this incredible journey!

CONTENTS

THE RICHEST
OF FOODS

In the early weeks of the year 2000, I felt a strong inner urging to set aside 40 days for fasting and prayer. This was to be the second such experience in my life. Inspired by a friend and mentor, Dr. Bill Bright, my first experience with such a prolonged fast in late 1996 was truly life changing. But I had quickly concluded after that first fast that my extensive travel demands made it quite unlikely that I would ever do it again. God had other ideas.

I was not sure what the focus of the second fast was to be. But our ministry was about to begin a large building project called The Jericho Center, and I felt we needed much more focused prayer to see this project properly launched. I determined my fast would continue from March 8 (Ash Wednesday) until Palm Sunday, April 16, in conjunction with a call to 40 days of fasting and prayer for America by Pray USA.

On the first noon of my fast, I joined with hundreds of other worshipers at the World Prayer Center in Colorado Springs. Beginning about two years earlier, these Wednesday worship times had grown from about 10 or 15 regular worshipers to standing room only, with hundreds of participants coming from many churches, ministries and businesses—even officers from the nearby United States Air Force Academy.[1]

Frankly, as I entered into that time of worship, joining with hundreds of others, I had difficulty getting my mind off myself—off the fact that this was but day 1 of 40. My stomach was grumbling and growling, already complaining in anticipation of the 39 days to follow. I thought more than once of Martin Luther's description of a season of fasting and prayer: "My flesh was wont to grumble dreadfully."

Yet, I felt it would be appropriate to begin my season of fasting and prayer in this worship atmosphere. Little could I have known how significant that decision would be. So there I was, trying my best to enter a worship mood while thinking of the many days of denial before me. It took at least 15 or 20 minutes before I affirmed inwardly that I was really there for one purpose—to focus my attention fully on the Lord.

Suddenly, the worship leader, who normally speaks very little during this unique hour, spoke a single Scripture, while he continued to play in a worshipful manner on the keyboard. It was that lone verse that was to launch me into one of my life's most extraordinary seasons of seeking God.

"As we worship," the leader declared, "let's think on these words of King David." Then he boldly read verse 5 of Psalm 63, "You satisfy me more than the richest of foods. I will praise you with songs of joy" (*NLT*).

I immediately found myself weeping. I knew the Lord was speaking; it was that familiar gentle whisper in my heart: "I'm not calling you to a season of fasting and prayer but to 40 days of fasting and worship."

The thought was new to me. I really could not remember hearing the words "fasting and worship" linked before. It had always been "fasting and prayer."

The impression continued. "Did I not commission my apostles Paul and Barnabas through fasting and worship?"

The Lord was bringing my mind back to Acts 13:2, where we read, "While [the early church leaders] were *worshiping the Lord and fasting,* the Holy Spirit said, 'Set apart for me Barnabas and Saul for the work to which I have called them'" (emphasis added).

I was later reminded of the powerful impact Paul and Barnabas had as they began a ministry that literally transformed cities and regions throughout Asia and Europe with the gospel. Consider these expressions: "Almost the whole city gathered to hear the word of the Lord" (Acts 13:44) and "The word of the Lord spread through the whole region" (v. 49). There was also great power in their preaching: "They spoke so effectively that a great number of Jews and Gentiles believed" (Acts 14:1). Of their ministry in Derbe we read: "They preached the good news in that city and won a large number of disciples" (v. 21).

DELIGHTS AND DESIRES

Fasting and worship, it seemed, clearly produced powerful results when linked to proclaiming the gospel. *Could worship be the key to transforming cities and nations today?* This thought flooded my mind as I entered those early moments of that first day of my worship fast.

As I continued worshiping with those World Prayer Center worshipers, my heart was flooded with additional Scripture—all providing direction for the coming 40 days.

First, there was a verse I had memorized years earlier as a teenager: "Delight yourself in the LORD and he will give you the desires of your heart" (Ps. 37:4). I felt the Lord asking me, "Isn't it your desire to see every nation on Earth touched with My love, home by home and family by family?"

My response, through tears, was an obvious yes. The ministry I lead, Every Home for Christ, clearly has this vision. I also realized that the challenge ahead of us for accomplishing this goal is formidable, especially in restricted areas like the Middle East and China.

The Lord continued speaking, "Doesn't my Word say that if you delight in Me, I will give you the desires of your heart?" The answer was equally obvious.

My heart then heard what was to be the beginning of the remarkable worship encounters that lay ahead for me during the 40-day fast: "I'm calling you to new heights of delight in Me during these 40 days!"

I knew God was speaking. An immediate impression followed: "For the next 40 days I want you to *sing* all your praise and prayers to Me, not just to *speak* them."

This was certainly unlike anything I had ever done over a sustained period. True, I had once spent an entire day in spontaneous singing to the Lord, which I described in the last chapter of my book *The Jericho Hour*. But that was with a roomful of other intercessors. This would be alone—and for 40 days.

As worship continued during that World Prayer Center encounter, I opened my Bible to meditate momentarily on Psalm 37:4, where we read about delighting in the Lord. Immediately my eyes caught a glimpse of a passage in the previous chapter. It further confirmed that God was leading me to new dimensions of delight in Him. I read, "All humanity finds shelter in the shadow of your wings. You feed them from the abundance of your own house, letting them drink from your rivers of delight" (Ps. 36:7-9, *NLT*). I mentally pictured myself at the edge of a glorious river of God's delight, drinking from it freely for the next 40 days!

My journey of joy was about to begin. It would take me to those new heights of delight God had promised me during that Wednesday worship experience. It would also confirm in me the profound significance of the role of intercessory worship—not only in evangelizing the world, quite literally, but also in transforming individuals, families, nations and entire people groups in the process.

The Key to Transformation

The pages that follow describe what I believe will be the key to this transformation movement. Worship, unlike anything the Church has ever experienced, along with resulting intercession at levels of authority few could have conceived of even a few years ago, will be that key. I believe this will bring about unified strategies of alliances and partnerships throughout Christ's Body that will be unparalleled in Church history—not just in evangelizing peoples and nations, but also in truly transforming them. A glorious worship awakening is on the global horizon and it's heading your way!

INTERCESSORY WORSHIP

A VISION OF AFRICA: HOLY SMOKE

I had a vision of Africa.

It flashed with such clarity that it has stayed on the front burner of my consciousness for months now, and I see the same picture again and again. As so often happens with such experiences, this vision-encounter seems to grow with intensity each time I contemplate it rather than fading with time.

It happened in Colorado Springs. It was mid-March and I was 10 days into a 40-day fast, praying over a team of intercessors and strategists preparing to go to Zimbabwe in Southern Africa.

The team planned to visit the famed Victoria Falls, discovered by British missionary-explorer David Livingstone in 1855, and then trek into interior regions to visit villages only now hearing the gospel, systematically, home by home and hut by hut. In addition to planting gospel booklets in the language of these villagers, the missionaries would use creative ways to witness to nonreaders. They were to carry large picture charts vividly depicting how Christ comes into a person's heart and drives away the dark, evil forces that those superstitious villagers feared and worshiped.

Suddenly, as we placed our hands on the shoulders of these worship warriors, I was momentarily transported mentally to the very region they would be visiting. I was in Africa, gazing from an elevated ridge far into the interior of the Zambezi River basin. I could see smoke rising from villages in almost every direction, thousands of them, perhaps tens of thousands.

Instantly, my mind reflected back to one of missions' most memorable statements of passion, voiced by Robert Moffat. It was 1839, and 26-year-old David Livingstone was at a meeting of the London Missionary Society. Moffat, home after an exhaustive missionary tenure in Africa, was pleading for would-be missionaries to pick up the mantle of missions and come to "the dark continent." Painting a word picture of the vast darkness of unevangelized Africa, Moffat declared:

> I have sometimes seen, in the morning sun, the smoke of a thousand villages where no missionary has ever been.[1]

Almost immediately Livingstone picked up Moffat's mantle and within 24 months had settled in Kuruman, Moffat's own field of witness. It was 1841. Three years later Livingstone was to marry Robert Moffat's daughter, Mary, and the rest of the story is remarkable missions history.

And so it was, a century and a half later, that I was mentally seeing a picture similar—or so it seemed—to the one Moffat saw in 1839.

I was looking at the smoke of *many thousands* of villages, not Moffat's "thousand."

"Lord," I said with concern, "are there yet that many villages where the gospel has not reached?"

"No," came the instant impression on my heart, "you are not seeing the smoke of the villages where the gospel has never been heard. You are seeing the smoke of the incense of worship rising from thousands and thousands of villages now transformed by My glory. You are seeing villages that have become worship centers of My presence."[2]

The team with which I was praying would soon discover that entire villages are now turning to Jesus in this present extraordinary season of global harvest. They would verify the research reports that Africa is truly experiencing spiritual awakening in spite of its obvious troubles. In the last century, the number of Christians in Africa increased 2,000 percent, from 9.9 million to 203 million. Each year, the continent has 6 million more Christians than it had the year before. "The rate of growth seems only to be increasing. In 1970, about 12 percent of Africans were Christians. Now, nearly half are," wrote Don Melvin in the *Minneapolis Star Tribune*. "In 1970 one-tenth of all Christians in the world were Africans. Now the continent is home to more than a fifth of the world's Christians."[3] The Lord was confirming in my heart that the already-expanding global harvest of people coming to Christ was soon to increase even more dramatically. Already we are seeing some isolated communities and cities being remarkably transformed, as highlighted powerfully by the popular *Transformation* videos produced from the research of George Otis Jr.[4] The day would come, I sensed, when entire nations would be transformed by the gospel, not merely "evangelized" in the sense that strategists can say the Church has "statistically" reached a nation with the gospel, but thoroughly transformed.

I was quickly convinced the smoke from these thousands of villages represented intercessory worship—a theme I believe will soon saturate Christ's Body globally.

INTERCESSORY WORSHIP: THE HARP AND BOWL

What is intercessory worship?[5] The term "intercessory worship," I believe, refers to concentrated worship that becomes intercessory in nature because it carries the prayers of God's people, like the fragrance of incense, before God's throne. As a result, God releases His power to accomplish His purposes for the harvest (see Rev. 5:8-10; 8:1-6).

A unique picture of intercessory worship can be seen in the harp and bowl symbols described in Revelation 5:8-10. Here we read:

And when [the Lamb] had taken [the scroll], the four living creatures and the twenty-four elders fell down before the Lamb. Each one had a harp and they were holding golden bowls full of incense, which are the prayers of the saints (v. 8).

Interestingly, the worshipers coming before the Lamb with harps in one hand (symbols of worship) and bowls in the other (symbols of prayer and intercession) seem to combine these two symbols in the release of a song never sung before. It is a song of global harvest. The text continues:

And they sang a new song: "You are worthy to take the scroll and to open its seals, because you were slain, and with your blood you purchased men for God from every tribe and language and people and nation" (v. 9).

It is not without significance that the harp and bowl picture here is linked to the redeemed coming from every tribe, language, people and nation. This clearly is a harvest song.

Later, in Revelation 8:1-6, we see "the prayers of all the saints" (a picture of intercession) being released with "much incense" (a picture of worship) at the throne. This release results in the final unfolding of God's plan through the sounding of seven trumpets, the last of which sounds a blast that releases a shout in heaven, declaring:

> The kingdom of the world has become the king-
> dom of our Lord and of his Christ, and he will
> reign for ever and ever (Rev. 11:15).

However we might interpret all this, we can be certain that worship-saturated intercession will be a key to
the last great harvest on Earth. To me, the harp and
bowl intercessory worship movement may well become
the greatest prayer movement in the history of the
Church.

Helping me understand the role of worship in fulfilling the Great Commission was John Piper's timely book
Let the Nations Be Glad. Piper wrote:

> Missions is not the ultimate goal of the church.
> Worship is. Missions exists because worship
> doesn't. Worship is ultimate, not missions,
> because God is ultimate, not man. When this age
> is over, and the countless millions of redeemed
> fall on their faces before the throne of God, mis-
> sions will be no more. It is a temporary necessity.
> But worship abides forever.[6]

In my unfolding journey to new heights of delight in God, I was quickly to discover the link between worship and intercession, the harp and the bowl, in God's plan for transforming nations. But for now it seemed the Lord wanted to especially highlight the harp side of the equation.

THE WORTH OF WORSHIP

A review of the whole matter of worship will prove worthwhile in laying a foundation for the insights that follow.

> Missions is not the ultimate goal of the Church. Worship is.

My purpose in sharing these pages is not merely to provide just one more book on worship to our already well-stocked devotional libraries. My objective is to describe how I believe the glory of God, released through worship-saturated intercession, will ultimately *transform* entire nations and people groups, including our family and neighbors. Let me begin with a personal definition of worship. To me, in a sentence, worship is any act, thought or expression of willful adoration that exalts and enthrones God, thereby defeating and dethroning Satan.

When intercession—prayerful intervention in the needs of others—is added, we have intercessory worship.

Our word "worship" is derived from the Old English word "weorthscipe," which means "to ascribe worth, to pay homage, to reverence or to venerate."[7] Worship focuses on the issue of worth or worthiness.

We also need to establish at the outset that worship is not merely some activity engaged in during a typical Sunday morning worship service; it is a lifestyle. It is the reason we live. A born-again believer is first and foremost a worshiper. A. W. Tozer said it succinctly, "We are called to an everlasting preoccupation with God."[8]

Even when describing revival, Tozer linked it to worship. He wrote, "Revival is a sudden bestowment of a spirit of worship upon God's people."[9]

We recall the words of the apostle Peter, "But you are a chosen people, a royal priesthood, a holy nation, a people belonging to God, that you may declare the praises of him who called you out of darkness into his wonderful light" (1 Pet. 2:9). As chosen people we are to "declare the praises" of God. The *King James Version* translates this phrase, "show forth the praises of him."

Worship, then, is both *how* we live and *why* we live. Tozer explains, "Worship of the loving God is man's whole reason for existence. That is why we were born and that is why we are born again from above. That is why we were created and that is why we have been recreated." This wise worshiper concludes, "That is also why there is a church. The Christian church exists to worship God first of all. Everything else must come second or third or fourth or fifth."[10]

Unfortunately, too often when discussing the theme of worship with the average believer, thoughts almost immediately focus on some kind of a church service worship-encounter. Some might imagine a less-than-exciting 20 minutes of rather lifeless liturgical worship. Others possibly picture a Sunday morning experience of standing for what seems to be an eternity singing for the tenth or twelfth time what Methodist prayer strategist Terry Tykel describes as a "wall song" (a typical praise chorus projected on a wall or large screen at the front of the church sanctuary).

While writing these thoughts, a friend of mine asked me if I knew the difference between a hymn and a praise chorus. I sensed a humorous anecdote coming, and I was right.

He told of an old farmer named John who lived with his wife Martha on a small farm some distance from the big city. They attended a traditional church nearby that had been there for several generations. John had heard about a new independent congregation growing remarkably in the city and told Martha he desired to visit the church sometime to see what it was like. Martha encouraged him to do so, but she didn't attend due to her recurring arthritis.

So, next Sunday, John went alone. Upon his return, his wife questioned him regarding how this big church differed from theirs.

John pondered momentarily and answered, "Well, for one thing, they sing praise choruses instead of hymns."

"What's the difference?" Martha queried.

John thought for a moment and responded, "Well, Martha, if I were to say, 'The cows are in the corn!' that would by a hymn." He added, "But if I were to say, 'The cows, Martha, the cows, the cows, the cows; the big cows, the little cows, the black cows, the brown cows, the cows, the cows, Martha, Martha, the cows are in the corn; the tall, big, high, ripe, yellow, corn, Martha, Martha, Martha'—that would be a praise chorus."

I chuckled, of course, realizing how different our views of worship styles sometimes can be. But the reality is that worship is much more than a musical style, it is a *lifestyle*. Worship must be a way of life.

And because worship is, as the old Westminster Catechism describes it, "the chief end of man," it also becomes the chief means to that end. Worship, indeed, is ultimate. When linked with intercession to the extent that such intercession itself is *a part of* and *flows directly from* that worship, it becomes intercessory worship. Out of intercessory worship there appears to develop a climate for the transformation of whole cities, nations and peoples. This brief book (the first in my *Delight* trilogy) is about this relationship of intercessory worship and worldwide harvest.[11] It is your invitation to new *heights of delight* in pursuing God's ways of transforming families, friends, neighborhoods—even whole cities and nations—through cultivating a worship awareness. Let's take a closer look.

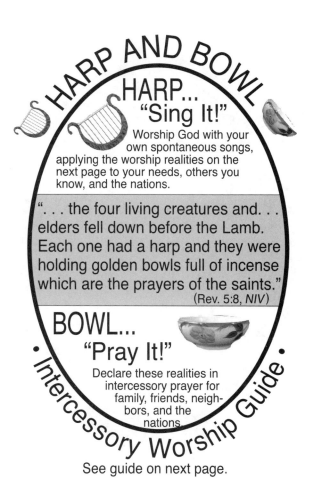

HARP AND BOWL

HARP...
"Sing It!"
Worship God with your own spontaneous songs, applying the worship realities on the next page to your needs, others you know, and the nations.

"...the four living creatures and... elders fell down before the Lamb. Each one had a harp and they were holding golden bowls full of incense which are the prayers of the saints." (Rev. 5:8, *NIV*)

BOWL...
"Pray It!"
Declare these realities in intercessory prayer for family, friends, neighbors, and the nations.

Intercessory Worship Guide

See guide on next page.

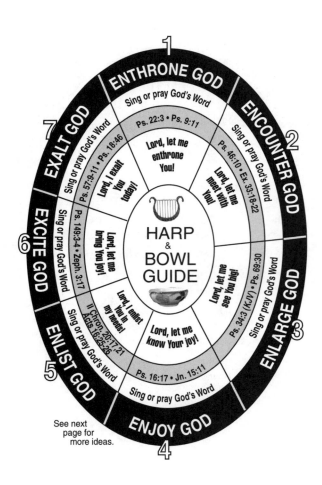

See next page for more ideas.

CULTIVATING YOUR "HARP AND BOWL"

Use these steps daily (with the guide opposite) to apply these intercessory worship realities. You can "sing it" (the harp) and "pray it" (the bowl). Compile your own list of Scriptures to sing or declare in prayer for each of the seven focuses. (The Scripture references on the opposite side will help you get started.)

	REALITY	PRINCIPLE	APPLICATION
1	Intercessory Worship **ENTHRONES GOD**	*Worship provides a place for God to dwell on earth in all his fullness.*	Declare in song (worship) and prayer (intercession) that God dwells in every situation.
2	Intercessory Worship **ENCOUNTERS GOD**	*Worship provides an opportunity to encounter God in all His fullness, first hand.*	Declare in song and prayer your desire to meet with God— then be still and wait in his presence.
3	Intercessory Worship **ENLARGES GOD**	*Worship provides an atmosphere to expand and increase our knowledge and understanding of God in all His fullness.*	Declare in song and prayer God's greatness in comparison to every attack of the enemy.
4	Intercessory Worship **ENJOYS GOD**	*Worship provides a place of entry into the delights and pleasures of God's presence.*	Declare in song and prayer your delight and joy in God for who He is and what He has done.
5	Intercessory Worship **ENLISTS GOD**	*Worship provides our primary means to mobilize and release the resources of God into the needs of people and nations.*	Declare in song and prayer that God's power is being released into your needs, and the nations.
6	Intercessory Worship **EXCITES GOD**	*Worship provides the only true position from which we might bring God pure pleasure.*	Declare in song and prayer your desire to excite the Lord through your worship and obedience.
7	Intercessory Worship **EXALTS GOD**	*Worship provides the platform and power necessary to exalt God in the nations.*	Declare in song and prayer that God is exalted over every need, opportunity and nation on earth.

WORSHIP ENTHRONES GOD

A BIG CHAIR FOR GOD

During my 40-day worship fast, I felt the Lord calling me not only to new delights in His presence but also to a clearer understanding of intercessory worship. As we learn to hold out our harps of worship together, with our bowls of intercessory prayer, we will make possible the completion of the Great Commission so all the world might experience God's glory, in Christ! Toward this end He showed me seven worship realities that I have come to describe as intercessory-worship principles.

Simply stated, a principle is a truth that is foundational to other truths. I believe an examination of these worship realities and related principles provides a meaningful place to begin understanding the role of worship, particularly intercessory worship, as it relates to the coming great ingathering of the last days' harvest.

Essential from the outset of our study is a critical recognition of what I feel is the first fundamental worship reality: *Worship enthrones God.* Stated more fully as an intercessory worship principle:

> ***Worship provides** a place for God to dwell on Earth in all His fullness.*

A HEAVENLY CLIMATE

In a uniquely profound way, the praises of God's people literally bring them into alignment with His throne and, thus, His full purposes and power. Said another way, God establishes His very throne in the physical place and among those people who are praising Him. This first worship reality is essential to our understanding of how and why worship is so vital to fulfilling God's purposes throughout the world. Worship creates a heavenly climate for the fulfillment of the Great Commission.

The psalmist declared, "Sing praises to the LORD, enthroned in Zion; proclaim among the nations what he has done" (Ps. 9:11). Here we note how the spirit of the Great Commission portrayed in this text ("proclaim among the nations") is linked in this statement with enthroning God—"Sing praises . . . enthroned . . . among the nations." It is not without significance that in the same admonition to sing praises to our Lord we see reference to proclaiming what the Lord has done among the nations.

Elsewhere, King David sang to the Lord, "But You are holy, enthroned in the praises of Israel" (Ps. 22:3, *NKJV*). The *King James Version* translates this verse, "Thou art holy, O thou that inhabitest the praises of Israel." The Hebrew word translated "inhabitest," *yawshab*, comes from a root word meaning "to sit." Of course, the place God sits is His throne, thus leading to the use of the expression "enthroned."

The thought here is that God literally dwells, reveals Himself, where His people praise Him. He inhabits that very place. I am told a Japanese translation of this verse reads, "When God's people praise Him, He brings a big chair and sits there."[1]

What a wonderful thought—and one that is clearly compatible with the original Hebrew expression. Our praises become God's throne—they literally *enthrone* Him.

Jack Hayford, discussing this same Scripture in his book *Worship His Majesty*, wrote:

> This oft-quoted statement from Psalm 22:3 deserves our greatest understanding, since the implications of the verb *yawshab* [inhabitest, *KJV*] are dramatic. Though the basic idea of the word is to sit down, when the King of the Universe is the subject, it is appropriately translated "enthroned." This great truth resounds to every generation: *Praise creates a dwelling place for God in man's present situation!*[2]

All of this is profoundly significant in our understanding of intercessory worship and its resulting enthronement of God, whether in our daily personal lives or in participating in the establishing of God's plan for the nations.

Worship enthrones God! This first worship reality suggests that when we begin declaring God's praises over our needs or distant nations, we are literally establishing His throne amid those needs or nations. God marches in, sits down, extends His scepter and intervenes as the King. Further, it is vital to realize that God and Satan cannot occupy the same space at the same time. Said simply, they don't sit well together—in fact, not at all. When God enters in, Satan must flee.

> When we begin declaring God's praises over our needs or distant nations, we are literally establishing His throne amid those needs or nations.

THE CASE OF CASEROS

This reality was uniquely illustrated in a recent event that involved Every Home for Christ (EHC).[3] A team of worshiping intercessors prayer-walked through the neighborhoods of their city in Argentina, the town of Caseros, declaring God's praises over each home in every neighborhood as they walked. They asked God to prepare the hearts of their neighbors to receive the Good News.

Caseros, with a population of 390,000, had been targeted for an Every Home campaign. But Caseros was not an easy place to evangelize because of the strong presence of various satanic cults, particularly those known as the Macumba and Umbanda. According to EHC's director there, Rino Bello, for every evangelical church in Caseros there are five or six satanic worship centers. Yet through his campaign, every family in almost 100,000 homes would be given a personal presentation of the gospel of Jesus Christ in their language, as well as an invitation to view Campus Crusade for Christ's *Jesus* film in one of several locations throughout the community.

Because satanic worship was prevalent in the city, seven churches of the city had been mobilized to walk the streets of Caseros, declaring the praises of God while interceding in prayer for every household. These churches had agreed to send teams of worshiping intercessors, the advance troops for a larger group of believers from at least 20 churches that would ultimately visit every home in the city, presenting to each a printed gospel message.

The overall strategy involved breaking up Caseros into several small districts, each of which was to be targeted one at a time. The first was an area called Villa Pineral and consisted of about 1,100 homes. First the prayer teams saturated the area with intercessory worship, and then, during a five-day period, every home in this area was personally visited and given a printed gospel message in their language, as well as an invitation to view the *Jesus* film.

UNDER THE OMBU TREE

The following Sunday evening, after the door-to-door evangelism had been completed, the *Jesus* film was shown in the public square of Villa Pineral. The large screen had been set up beneath a huge 200-year-old ombu tree, considered a treasured historic site in the community. At the conclusion of the the film, 135 people gave their hearts to Jesus. This was in addition to the many who had responded as the result of the home-to-home evangelism.

Showing the film under the huge ombu tree was especially significant because for almost a decade this unique tree had been the site of area-wide satanic worship gatherings every week. Friday night was the time specifically set aside by satanic worshipers to bring their sacrifices to Satan. (Quite often these sacrifices included body parts of animals such as chickens, cats and dogs.)

The choice to proclaim the gospel in this particular place set the stage for a spiritual confrontation in the heavenlies, as well as an occasion for evangelism. This became apparent in the days immediately following the Sunday-night showing of the film.

That following Tuesday, without any plausible explanation, the 200-year-old ombu tree mysteriously "exploded" and split in half, falling to the ground. The noise was heard many blocks away. The city engineer, with two of his colleagues, came to examine the fallen tree. It had no visible disease, nor was there any bad weather at the time, or lightning, that might account for this strange occurrence.

Those believers involved in the campaign who had heard the sound and witnessed the fallen tree knew it was an act of God. Our Every Home for Christ director explained, "We understood that this tree had fallen as the result of spiritual warfare against the powers of darkness. We knew that God had ordered this to happen as an indication that revival was on its way and that many lost souls would be won to Christ."

But God was not finished yet. These believers were to see a further sign of the impact of their intercessory worship over Caseros. Exactly one month to the day following the first explosion, a second explosion took place—at the exact site where the mighty ombu once stood. This time the very roots of the 200-year-old tree exploded under the ground. If the first explosion was unusual, the second was bizarre!

Later we learned that immediately after the first explosion, one of the satanic leaders in Caseros had admonished his followers to go to the site of the fallen ombu tree and dig up some of its roots so that the original tree, sacred to the satanists, might be planted and regrown. Thus, a new point of worship for their cult might be established.

A woman in this cult had responded and was collecting roots at the time of the second explosion. As she lay on the ground severely injured, waiting for an ambulance, a television crew from a national TV network in Argentina came and filmed what had happened. The story was televised that night across the region.

The news report showed the lady being rushed to the hospital where she lay in grave condition. At first it was thought she might not survive. Her neighbor, a committed Christian, recognized the injured woman from the television report and decided to visit her in the hospital. In an amazing turn of events, this satanist who had attempted to dig up the ombu roots received Christ as Savior and totally renounced all ties to the satanic cult.

Soon, many others received Christ in the city of Caseros.

In the weeks following the two strange explosions, other interesting testimonials emerged from the churches of Caseros. Members of one church reported that for many years it was common to find parts of sacrificed animals on their church doorstep on Sunday mornings. But after the second explosion of the old ombu tree, those occurrences abruptly stopped.

A THEOLOGY OF GOD'S PRESENCE

There is little doubt that those teams of worshiping intercessors who walked the streets of Caseros in intercessory worship had enthroned God in their community. The results speak for themselves and validate our first reality. Worship, indeed, provides a place for God to dwell among His people and thereby brings Him into their circumstances in all His fullness. This unleashes explosive potential for the transformation of communities, peoples and even entire nations.

But how do we explain more adequately what transpires when we enthrone God over a situation or region? Tommy Tenney, author of *The God Chasers* as well as the timely *God's Favorite House*, suggests, "There is a theology of God's presence. When His manifested presence (as opposed to His omnipresence) appears in any area or vicinity, the forces of darkness lose their ability to sway the public."[4]

Tenney's reference to God's *manifest presence* compared to His *omnipresence* is the simple reality that although God is always present (His omnipresence), He sometimes chooses to manifest Himself in much more of His glory (His manifest presence). God is always present; it is just that we do not always sense or recognize this fact. Sadly, a survey by researcher George Barna revealed that 7 out of 10 Christians said they have never felt God's presence while attending church.[5]

In this regard we might define God's presence in three ways—God's *intellectual* presence, God's *conscious* presence and God's *manifest* presence. We use these terms to describe how we as believers might view God's presence, not necessarily how God views the reality of His own presence, or existence.

By referring to God's *intellectual* presence, I mean our intellectual recognition that God exists everywhere and therefore He must be present. This would fall into Tenney's description of God's omnipresence. Faith necessitates this belief that He is present. Because we believe God is everywhere, therefore He is here!

This fact was uniquely emphasized to me when I was preparing to leave on a ministry trip many years ago from California to Washington, D.C. Our two daughters, Dena and Ginger, were just six and three years old, respectively. It was my custom to go into their bedroom the night before a trip and sit between them on their bed while each prayed a simple prayer. I asked Dena if she would pray first, specifically asking that God would be with me on my trip.

I could tell Dena was thinking about something because of the pause before she prayed. Then, with a quizzical look, the six-year-old queried, "Daddy, can I ask you a question?"

"Sure," I replied.

"Why should I ask God to do something for you that He has already promised to do anyway?"

I was, of course, momentarily dumbfounded, and choked out some sort of answer like, "Well, Dena, that's true, but it still never hurts to ask." Meanwhile I was thinking, *Oh dear, we have a six-year-old theologian on our hands!*

Intellectually, we know God is present. Yet there are times when we *sense* His presence in such a way that we both know and feel He is near. We might describe this as His *conscious* presence because we consciously feel He is present. John Wesley described his conversion with the expression, "My heart was strangely warmed." Of course, Wesley's conversion would have been just as real even without that warm feeling, but he was sensing something. To a degree, this is what we might consider the *conscious* presence of God.

The *manifest* presence of God is something far more intense, though it also involves a sense, or feeling, of God's being near. Though not always the case, God's manifest presence generally has a sweeping impact, touching many people—even whole communities or regions—not merely a single individual. Real revival is frequently—if not always—the result of the *manifest* presence of God upon His people.

As weak an explanation as this may be, it is worth exploring. And by exploring I mean experiencing, rather than merely studying. But for now we will have to be content with planting seeds for your future experiential exploration.

ENTERING GOD'S THRONE ZONE

Tommy Tenney amplifies our first reality—that worship enthrones God, especially as it relates to God's manifest presence and a resulting harvest of souls—by introducing the concept of God's "throne zone"! Tenney writes:

> A friend of mine coined the term, "throne zone,"
> to describe the atmosphere of worship that goes
> on around the throne of God. If somehow we can
> recreate the throne zone on earth as it is in heav-
> en in our churches and meetings, if our worship
> becomes so compelling that the manifest pres-
> ence of God begins to put itself on display in our
> midst, then we will see the glory of God begin to
> flow through our cities. When this happens, the
> lost will come to Christ on a massive scale that we
> have never seen before.[6]

It appears that most revivals and awakenings began as small streams where the manifest presence of God had begun to flow. Soon those streams became rivers. The Welsh Revival began with a coal miner turned preacher, Evan Roberts, sharing the brokenness of his heart to a few people who stayed late after a Monday-night prayer meeting.

America's Great Awakening of the mid-1850s began at a noon prayer meeting at the Old Dutch North Church on Fulton Street in New York City. Only six people had gathered for an hour of prayer, including a layman,

Jeremiah Lamphier, who called the first meeting. Within 2 years, tens of thousands were praying weekly in cities across America's East Coast, resulting in 50,000 new conversions to Christ every week, a conversion rate that was sustained for months.

Although all such awakenings have had differing manifestations, each seemed to result from an intensely fervent passion for God coming upon His people. Deep repentance, for example, came when people wanted nothing between them and God that would hinder their worship. Fervent united prayer was primarily focused on seeking God so that He would simply "come!"

Today's growing harp and bowl intercessory worship movement is precisely this, possibly taken to new heights in the pursuit of God. And you can join this movement daily. It's simple:

> *Declare in song (worship) and prayer (intercession) that God dwells, or is enthroned, in every situation.*

This is the result of all this intercessory worship: God *is* being enthroned because His people *are* pursuing Him in passionate worship as never before. Throne zones *are* being established throughout the earth where God can dwell in all His fullness. Radical, revolutionary intercession is the result, and a new climate is being created to transform peoples and nations through fruitful evangelism. And this is only the beginning.

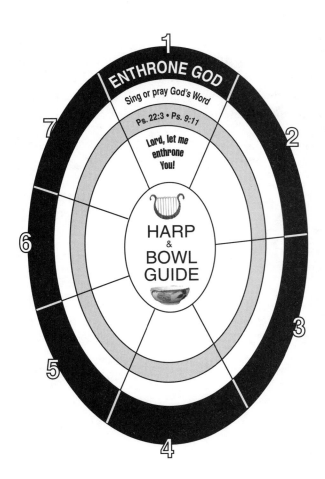

1

ENTHRONE GOD

Sing or pray God's Word

Ps. 22:3 • Ps. 9:11

Lord, let me
enthrone
You!

HARP
&
BOWL
GUIDE

7

2

6

3

5

4

WORSHIP ENCOUNTERS GOD

A FEW KIND WORDS FOR SILENCE

"You must begin with God. Then you begin to understand everything in its proper context. All things fit into shape and form when you begin with God," wrote A. W. Tozer, one of the great worship mentors of the past century. He defined "genius" well when he wrote, "The wisest person in the world is the person who knows the most about God.

The only real sage worthy of that name is the one who realizes that the answer to creation and life and eternity is a theological answer—not a scientific answer."[1]

Tozer brings us to our second vital worship reality in recognizing the relationship between intercessory worship and the ultimate transformation of nations: *Worship encounters God.*

One might wonder why this reality is not first on our list since it could be argued that we cannot enthrone God until we first encounter Him. However, I am not speaking here of that initial encounter we have of God in Christ, at conversion, but rather of those ongoing intimate encounters that leave us wanting much, much more.

From these experiences we begin to develop a passion to see others, even multitudes, brought into these same encounters as they first meet and then grow in Christ. Thus, this worship reality again leads directly to the harvest and the ultimate transformation of peoples and nations.

Stated as our second intercessory worship principle:

Worship provides an opportunity to encounter God in all His fullness, firsthand.

ASTONISHED REVERENCE

Encountering God is clearly basic to all true worship and is certainly essential to powerful intercession. And at the heart of encountering God is a pure, passionate adoration and fear of God.

Tozer, whom I quote often on this subject because worship was his life, explains,

> I will say that when we adore God, all the beautiful ingredients of worship are brought to white, incandescent heat with the fire of the Holy Spirit. To adore God means we love him with all the powers within us. We love him with fear and wonder and yearning and awe.[2]

Notice Tozer's reference to fear as it relates to our encounters with God. There is a significant difference between anxious fear and godly fear. Providing an example, Tozer tells us of how the apostle John reacted in the garden of Gethsemane (see John 18) when Jesus was arrested. John was among those who ran away in *fear*. He was no doubt afraid of being arrested. Tozer suggests it was either a fear of danger, a fear of punishment or a fear of humiliation. But later, when John was exiled on Patmos (see Rev. 1:12-17), he saw an awesome Being standing amid golden lamp stands and experienced an entirely different kind of fear.

Tozer observes that in this situation, John is not afraid and he does not feel threatened. He is, in fact, experiencing godly fear. Thus, a true fear of God is a beautiful thing, for it includes worship, love and veneration all at once. It is encountering God! Tozer concludes: "True worship is to be so personally and hopelessly in love with God that the idea of a transfer of affection never even remotely exists. That is the meaning of the fear of God."[3]

Interestingly, earlier in this same work by Tozer, the author describes this fear and wonder of God as a part of a "sweet relationship" and "astonished reverence": "When we come into this sweet relationship, we are beginning to learn astonished reverence, breathless adoration, awesome fascination, lofty admiration of the attributes of God and something of the breathless silence that we know when God is near." The author adds, "You may never have realized that before, but all of those elements in our perception and consciousness of the Divine Presence add up to what the Bible calls 'the fear of God.'"[4]

Absolute silence might well become, in some instances, our greatest act of worship. Tozer referred to our experiencing a "breathless silence" when we know God is near. Not all worship is expressed in words or actions. Indeed, the closer one comes to a true encounter with God, the less appropriate some words or actions become. Our very silence can have a uniquely profound impact on extending God's kingdom throughout the nations.

Note God's dramatic admonition regarding silence. God commands, "Be silent, and know that I am God! I will be honored by every nation. I will be honored throughout the world" (Ps. 46:10, *NLT*). Here we discover that being silent in God's presence, as an act of worship, is linked to impacting the nations, and it is certainly essential to "knowing" God, for the text clearly implies that being silent leads to a deeper knowledge of God.

THE LOST ART OF WORSHIP

All of this brings us back to our second premise, that worship provides the opportunity for us to encounter God in all His fullness, firsthand. Of course, to encounter God is to know Him—up close!

In Proverbs we read, "The reverence and fear of God are basic to all wisdom. Knowing God results in every other kind of understanding" (Prov. 9:10, *TLB*). The *New International Version* reads, "Knowledge of the Holy One is understanding." A. W. Tozer, who also wrote the classic book *The Knowledge of the Holy*, wisely said, "The Christian is strong or weak, depending upon how closely he has cultivated a knowledge of God."[5]

Especially significant is the verse, "Knowing God results in every other kind of understanding." The word "every" is an all-encompassing adjective. All the wisdom we could possibly need is reserved for those who increase their knowledge of God. And according to the Word of God to the psalmist, silence and knowing God are linked— "Be silent, and know that I am God!"

This seems a good occasion to offer a few kind words for silence. Silence is a lost art of focused worship in much of the Church today. And sadly, where there is a measure of it, it is but a small fragment of an otherwise lifeless liturgy.

Worshipful silence takes time and incredible discipline. In the last decade I have not been in any typical worship setting where more than a token moment was devoted to pure silence. And when such a time was appointed, it was usually designated for silent prayer, which suggests our minds are still very active—we are just praying under our breath. But, silence implies that nothing is happening, and our human nature cries out for things to happen—even in worship.

Silence, however, when properly understood and cultivated, is a power all by itself if God is encountered in the process. Listen again to Tozer: "More spiritual progress can be made in one short moment of speechless silence in the awesome presence of God than in years of mere study."[6]

> More spiritual progress can be made in one short moment of speechless silence in the awesome presence of God than in years of mere study.

THE OIL OF EXPECTANCY

I am not good at silence. I think that is why God acted as He did in my personal journey to amplify the importance of this worship reality.

A year prior to my 40-day worship-fast in December 1998, I felt strongly led to set aside an entire month to seek God regarding Every Home for Christ's emerging 10-year plan (2000–2010), called Completing the Commission.[7] The plan included our goal of fulfilling our ministry mandate of reaching every home on Earth with the gospel by December 31, 2010.

But the more I studied the complexity and cost of the plan, the more I realized it was clearly impossible without a miracle beyond anything any of us could ever imagine.

This was to be the second such month-long prayer experience for me. The first occurred in December of 1987 when God burdened my heart with the great need for the gospel in Communist Eastern Europe and the Soviet Union.

Those prayers in 1987 were remarkably answered, and since that time Every Home for Christ has visited and given the printed gospel to more than 40 million households over a 10-year period in just this Eurasian region alone. Nearly 2 million people from the former Soviet Union and Eastern Europe have mailed a decision card or written a letter requesting information about Jesus. The majority indicated they had received Christ as Savior.

Prior to that time, the number of such requests was probably fewer than 200 in more than two decades from the entire region.

So, here I was about to enter my second month-long prayer experience. As with my first month of prayer, I felt specifically led to set aside the amount of time daily for prayer that I would normally spend in my office or in planning meetings and preaching assignments. I did not feel it was to be a time of fasting and prayer, as such, but rather a full month of seeking God (sometimes with others)—every day.

For this second month-long commitment, I decided to keep a daily calendar and on selected days invite other intercessors, as well as our staff, to join me for prayer. Among other focuses for the month, for two days we specifically prayed over and anointed with oil the 10-year plan that had prompted this month of prayer in the first place.

Much of these two days was spent literally on our faces in my office. At one point we anointed each of the hundreds of pages of the plan with traditional anointing oil. On the third day, all of our staff spent a day doing the same thing. It was truly a symbolic saturation of the plan with the oil of expectancy and anticipation, and to this day I keep this copy of the plan, with oil marks on each page, in my prayer room at home.

BEEN THERE, DONE THAT

The rest of that month held an interesting variety and diversity of prayer experiences. But by Sunday, December 20, a little "warrior weariness" had set in. That night as I sat alone in my prayer closet under the staircase in our basement, I quietly wondered, *What should I do next?* I remember telling the Lord, "I'm not sure if there's anything else I can do to seek You this month that I haven't already done, probably five or six times."

This was not an arrogant statement, but an honest expression of losing steam in my praying. Of course, I knew better, but still there was something of a "been there, done that" feeling. My heart was crying out, "I've run out of ideas, God, and it's only December 20. I've got 11 days to go in this month of prayer and I'm dying down here!"

That is when it happened. As clearly as you read these words on this page, the gentle whisper of God's unmistakable voice filled my mind. It was soft but firm.

No! You haven't done everything, the voice said. *There is at least one thing you've never done in my presence for an entire day*.

For a moment I honestly did not know what the Lord was referring to. What had I never done in prayer for an entire day?

My mind searched my past prayer encounters that had lasted a complete day. I remembered an entire day simply praising God. I also remembered how, on another occasion, I had spent a day just lying on my face before God. I had felt led to spend that day thanking God, by name, for every person who had ever blessed me. It was, to be sure, a day of many tears and incredible gratitude.

Then there was that most memorable day in 1987 when a handful of intercessors and I sang to the Lord for an entire day, spontaneously, in worship. None of these occasions had been planned because we had hoped to impress God, like climbing a spiritual Mt. Everest. Nor was it because we thought such dedication would prove that we were spiritual giants. These days resulted simply from a desire to get closer to God.

But now, on this twentieth day of my second month-long commitment, I wondered what I had missed. What had I never done for an entire day? What I heard next stunned me.

The gentle voice returned, *You've never spent an entire day in total silence in My presence.*

God clearly had me on that one! Actually, I had never even spent a single hour in total silence. (Make that 20 minutes!) Silence is just too tough and, frankly, a little unmanly. At least, that was my thinking.

Praying prostrate, claiming Scripture, singing praises, breaking strongholds, rebuking Satan—that is where the action is in prayer. *Silence is for sissies,* I reasoned. *And besides, what good would a full day of silence accomplish anyway?*

Then, God amazed me with His Word. He asked, *Is it not the desire of your heart and ministry to help reach all the unevangelized peoples of the earth with the Good News?* My response was, obviously, yes.

God's still small voice then questioned, *Does not My Word declare, "Be still, and know that I am God; I will be exalted among the nations, I will be exalted in the earth"?* (Ps. 46:10).

In that moment I began to weep as I saw the connection between pure, worshipful silence in God's presence and His being exalted in the *nations*. I could never remember reading or hearing someone suggest that simple, focused silence in God's presence was in any way connected to God being exalted in the nations through the completion of the Great Commission.

Instantly I knew I had to set aside just such a day of silence that month. I determined to do it three days later, on Wednesday, because I had already scheduled Monday and Tuesday to pray with others.

A GATHERING OF GENERALS

The next day, Monday, I took my monthly prayer emphasis to the nearby office of Generals of Intercession, headed by Mike and Cindy Jacobs. Cindy, an intercessor's intercessor, had heard about my month-long prayer focus and had invited me to join their staff that day for their usual monthly day of prayer. Little could I have known how significant this visit to Cindy's office would be. God would use it to confirm what He had told me just the night before about the power of silence.

Cindy knew nothing of my Sunday-night encounter as Dee and I arrived for prayer at her office that Monday morning. After spending several hours in prayer, Cindy placed a huge map of our town of Colorado Springs on the floor of their prayer room. We sat in a circle around the large map, ready to do whatever Cindy suggested.

Cindy walked to a nearby table that held six giant-sized, four-inch-thick binders. Cindy reached for one, opened it, and placed it on the large map of our city. I recognized the binders. They contained a remarkable strategic listing of more than 6,000 unreached people groups, featuring specific details about each group, including geographic location, language and whether any evangelistic effort had been made.

I recognized the study because an exact set of similar binders had been given to Every Home for Christ. Frank Kaleb-Jensen of Adopt-A-People Clearing House knew of our strong commitment to mobilize Christ's Body to visit every dwelling, home by home, in all of these people groups, introducing each family to the gospel. So he gave us the complete set. Frank had also given a rare set of this unpublished listing to Generals of Intercession because of their commitment to mobilize massive, focused prayer for these unevangelized peoples.

Placing one of the large open binders on the map of our city, Cindy explained, "When Generals came to the Springs, we moved here because the Holy Spirit gave us a promise that somehow, from this community, we would help ultimately touch all these peoples with the gospel. Today I feel we are to put this binder on the map as a symbol of every unreached people group in the world and ask God to show us anything necessary to help us see this become a reality."

I could hardly hold back the tears. Only the night before God had clearly spoken to my heart, calling me to set aside an entire day of silence for the very purpose of seeing all the peoples of the earth touched with the Good News. "Be still," He told me, through His Word. "I will be exalted among the nations" (Ps. 46:10).

Excitedly, I told the intercessors about my experience the night before and of my planned day of silence scheduled for that Wednesday. It was to become one of the most special times of waiting in God's presence I was ever to experience.

AN ISAIAH ENCOUNTER

I vividly recall the start of that Wednesday encounter of silence. After several hours of simply being still, during which I battled the myriad rushing thoughts that often seemed much louder than if I had spoken them—or even shouted them—I suddenly sensed a uniquely open heaven. Although I was not specifically seeking to hear from the Lord, His voice spoke with unusual clarity, giving me details I had not thought of before on how our plan to reach the world's unreached peoples, home by home, would unfold.

Though space does not allow for the sharing of all these details here, I am convinced my Psalm 46:10 encounter of silence was crucial to unlocking an understanding of this vital reality. I knew this plan would find its fulfillment through strategic ministry alliances of many evangelism and discipleship organizations, along with business and professional leaders, all coming together to partner through intercessory worship.

All of this, of course, involves encountering God, a clear result of worship. And a fundamental key to encountering God is silence, which, as stated before, provides an opportunity to encounter God in all His fullness, *firsthand*. Silence, I was certain, would be a powerful key, because it is impossible to boast when you are truly silent. In fact, the very miracle at Jericho with the 12 tribes uniting to take the city was first and foremost a miracle of silence (see Josh. 6).

Every believer ought to seek God for an Isaiah encounter—something that can come only by spending significant time in God's presence (see Isa. 6:1-8). A season of silent anticipation is the place to begin. In Isaiah's case at least four things resulted.

First came *revelation*. Isaiah "saw the Lord seated on a throne, high and exalted" (6:1). This is the key that begins the process of experiencing all God has for us. The Hebrew word for "saw" here in Isaiah 6:1 means "to see something up close and clearly." Isaiah's was a crystal-clear encounter.

The apostle Paul would later speak of just such a revelation as he described his prayers for Ephesian believers. Paul related, "I keep asking that the God of our Lord Jesus Christ . . . may give you the Spirit of wisdom and revelation, so that you may know him better" (Eph. 1:17).

Second came *repentance*. Every true encounter with God leaves the believer with an awe and reverence for God's presence that creates a longing to be pure before Him. This is clear from Isaiah's exclamation: "'Woe to me!' I cried. 'I am ruined! For I am a man of unclean lips . . . and my eyes have seen the King'" (Isa. 6:5). We will not turn from that which is unholy if we do not recognize its unholiness. Isaiah's encounter confronted the prophet at his point of need, and he acknowledged it.

Third came *restoration*. One of the glorious angelic beings Isaiah pictures, a seraph, brings a live coal from God's altar and touches the prophet's mouth. The angel declares, "'See, this has touched your lips; your guilt is taken away and your sin atoned for'" (6:7). Isaiah experiences an immediate personal restoration.

Finally came *response*. As is often the case with such encounters, God now speaks clearly to the prophet, calling him to a lifelong prophetic ministry that would provide for us one of the great books of the Bible, the book bearing Isaiah's name. God asks the prophet, "'Whom shall I send? And who will go for us?'" (6:8).

Isaiah's response has been the text of countless missionary challenges: "'Here am I. Send me!'" (6:8).

How might we apply this Isaiah encounter and our second worship reality daily? May I suggest:

> *Declare in song and prayer your desire to meet with God—then be still and wait in His presence.*

APOSTOLIC WHISPERS

Worship, indeed, encounters God. And persistent worshipers will encounter God the most deeply.

Years ago I recall reading about the life of Francis of Assisi, one of the few bright lights shining in quite possibly the darkest days of the Church—the Middle Ages. The absence of light during that season was such that even historians refer to the period as the Dark Ages.

Once, while deep in prayer, it is said that Francis heard the audible voice of Christ. The voice said simply, "Go, Francis, and repair my House."

One of Francis of Assisi's biographers would later write, "From then on Francis could never keep himself from weeping."

Thomas of Celano, a Franciscan friar and poet, said: "He was always occupied with Jesus; Jesus he bore in his heart, Jesus in his mouth, Jesus in his ears, Jesus in his eyes, Jesus in his hands, Jesus in the rest of his members."[8]

Those who have studied the life of Francis of Assisi know he was first and foremost a worshiper. So remarkable was the impact of his life over so many generations that we can refer to him simply by the name of the Italian city in which he was born, Assisi, and most of the Church knows exactly who we are talking about.

This apostle of worship encountered God to such a degree—and so often—that some say his face literally glowed with God's presence when he came from his usual place of prayer. Oh, that God would raise up a new order of just such apostolic worshipers!

Silence was almost a creed with Francis of Assisi. He understood that words are not the underlying reality, either in worship or in witness. One memorable statement attributed to Francis, said to have been repeated often as a challenge to the brothers of his order, was: "Go everywhere and preach the gospel to everyone. And if you absolutely must, use words."[9]

Francis of Assisi, indeed, was a person of few words but a man of much power. Francis encountered God often, it is said, during whole days of almost total silence in a cave near Averno, Italy. From those worship encounters, Francis went forth as a mighty intercessor, a spiritual go-between, to impact entire generations of would-be worshipers.

Could it be that God is ready to raise up just such an entire generation of worshiping intercessors? Imagine an army of apostolic Francises, filled with God's Spirit, ready to transform whole neighborhoods, nations and the entire world with the gospel. Sound appealing? Then continue with me on this journey.

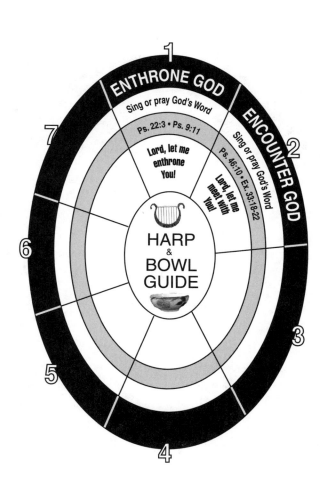

WORSHIP ENLARGES GOD

SEEING GOD BIG

Amplifying the necessity of a worship-saturated world-view, John Piper writes, "God is calling us above all else to be the kind of people whose theme and passion is the supremacy of God in all of life." To see God as supreme is to see God *big*. Piper wisely adds, "No one will be able to rise to the magnificence of the missionary cause who does not feel the magnificence of Christ. There will be no big world vision without a big God."[1]

These thoughts bring us to a profound truth in our understanding of the role of worship in fulfilling Christ's mandate to take the gospel to all peoples. The more we worship God, the bigger God becomes in our understanding, resulting in a greater faith to believe He will accomplish His purposes through us. Identified as our third worship reality: *Worship enlarges God!*

Of course, our worship does not actually change anything in or about God. To suggest that worship enlarges God really means it increases our capacity to know and understand Him in all His greatness. Tozer said it well: "You can't make God big. But you can see Him big."[2]

The psalmist prayerfully pleaded, "Oh, magnify the LORD with me, and let us exalt His name together" (Ps. 34:3, *NKJV*). Later in the psalms we read, "I will praise the name of God with a song, and will magnify Him with thanksgiving" (Ps. 69:30, *NKJV*).

The psalmist longed to discover God in all His greatness. He wanted to see God big, which is at the heart of our third intercessory worship principle:

Worship provides an atmosphere to expand and increase our knowledge and understanding of God in all His fullness.

A BAPTISM OF WONDER

We recall Mary's beautiful song, recorded in Luke and often referred to as the *Magnificat*. Mary said, "'My soul *magnifies* the Lord, and my spirit has rejoiced in God my Savior'" (Luke 1:46-47, *NKJV*, emphasis added). Mary was magnifying the Lord, as had the psalmist. She was seeing God *big* through her worship, an activity that could continue endlessly throughout eternity because God's magnificence is infinite.

When the power of God's Spirit came upon the house of Cornelius, the Bible says that those who observed this outpouring "heard them [Cornelius and his household] speak with tongues and magnify God" (Acts 10:46, *NKJV*). Here we discover that the same outpouring that had taken place on the Day of Pentecost among the Jews also occurred at the house of Cornelius among the Gentiles. As the Holy Spirit came, the worshipers began to *see God bigger* through their praise. All who were present were filled with awe and wonder.

A. W. Tozer speculated on what such a modern-day baptism of wonder might accomplish in transforming cultures. He wrote,

> In the very midst of the myriad of created wonders all around us, we have almost unknowingly

lost the capacity to wonder. If the Holy Spirit should come again upon us as in earlier times, visiting church congregations with the sweet but fiery breath of Pentecost, we would be greater Christians and holier souls. Beyond that, we would also be greater poets and greater artists and greater lovers of God and of His universe.[3]

Seeing God bigger also means understanding Jesus better. Joseph Garlington highlights this reality in his book *Worship: The Pattern of Things in Heaven*. Discussing how worship will help us see Jesus more clearly, Garlington suggests:

Although Jesus Christ won't be "better" than He is now, our understanding of Him, our comprehension of His love and sacrifice, our revelation of Him as God incarnate, and especially our capacity to enjoy intimate fellowship with Him will be better, fuller, richer, bigger, and deeper than what we have now.[4]

A PLANE OR A PEW

Max Lucado, in his inspiring book *Just Like Jesus*, addresses this theme of seeing God big in a section titled "A Worship-

Hungry Heart."[5] He does this uniquely by comparing people on a plane with people in a pew. According to Max, they
have a lot in common, a thought that occurred to him on
a flight one day. Most are well behaved and presentable;
some nod off, while others gaze out the window. There is
usually a certain satisfaction with the "predictable experience." When the worship service or flight is over, Max says,
you will hear the word "nice" quite frequently: "It was a *nice*
flight." "It was a *nice* worship service."

But a few, the author suggests, want more than "nice."
Like the little boy Max had just passed in the aisle who
boldly asked a flight attendant, "Will they really let me meet
the pilot?"

Fortunately, he made his request just as he passed the
cockpit door and the pilot heard him. He leaned out and
asked, "Someone looking for me?"

Shooting his hand high, the lad said, "I am," and was
promptly invited in. When he emerged a little later, his eyes
were wide with wonder. Excitedly he exclaimed, "Wow, I'm
so glad to be on this plane."

According to Max, most everyone else on the flight
was simply content. What they sought, they got. The boy,
however, wanted more. And he got it, too.

Lucado uses this story to define worship. He writes:

Worship is the act of magnifying God. Enlarging our vision of Him. Stepping into the cockpit to see where He sits and observe how He works. Of course, His size doesn't change, but our perception of Him does. As we draw nearer He seems larger. Isn't that what we need? A *big* view of God? Don't we have *big* problems, *big* worries, *big* questions? Of course we do. Hence we need a big view of God.[6]

STUDY THE LIGHT

Of course, in all of this we need to understand that seeing God bigger requires our knowing Jesus better. And this must go far beyond mere head knowledge to become a passionate heart yearning. We must pursue this study of Jesus by being *with* Him, long and often, not just by reading or hearing *about* Him.

An interesting lesson from a unique study of more than 2,000 years of lighthouse technology amplifies this thought. The study appeared in *Smithsonian* magazine, in an article titled "Science Makes a Better Lighthouse Lens."[7] According to the author, Bruce Watson, there were no major improvements in lighthouses from about 280 B.C., when the famed lighthouse of Alexandria, Egypt, towered

450 feet above Egypt's greatest harbor, until the mid-1800s. Even though many scientists and engineers tried their best to design and build a better lighthouse, they failed.[7]

Throughout most of those years, lighthouses burned coal or wood. Finally, by the eighteenth century, oil lamps with mirrors offered a little more light. Still, according to Watson, the shorelines of the world were littered with the ribs of rotting ships as evidence that little had improved in lighthouse technology over those 2,000 years. True, the glass lantern of the 1690s helped a little, as did the use of mirrors placed in huge, wooden bowls to create crude reflectors. But as maritime traffic increased, so did ship-wrecks. The quest was on for a far more reliable light source.

The goal of that quest was reached through the vision-ary genius of Augustin Fresnel, a frail, 34-year-old French-Swiss scientist who had a passion for optics, the branch of physics that studies how light behaves. Fresnel took a total-ly different approach from all the others who were seeking to build a better lighthouse. While others had tried to improve lighthouse technology, Fresnel decided simply to study the behavior of light itself. His studies not only advanced the understanding of the nature of light but also led to huge breakthroughs in the effectiveness of lighthouses.

In his study of light Fresnel developed a number of formulas to calculate the way light changes direction, or refracts, while passing through glass prisms. This led to the development of the remarkable Fresnel lens and, in the process, to a much better lighthouse. Fresnel arranged different lenses and dozens of prisms at precise angles so that diffuse lamplight was redirected into a unified, far-reaching beam.

Today, the concepts behind Fresnel's original lens impact our lives every time we turn on our automobile headlights. That is because headlights use adaptations of a Fresnel lens. A lens in a television studio camera is often referred to as a Fresnel lens. In fact, Fresnel's theories of light form the basis of all modern optics.

There is a lesson in all of this for those who would seek to be better worshiping intercessors. We need to study the Light, Christ Himself, if we truly want to see God bigger. Where light shines, we see more clearly. If we want to see God bigger, we need to see Christ more brightly!

MAKING SATAN SMALL

Interestingly, seeing God bigger through worship leads to bigger and more powerful prayers. The most effective intercessors I have known have cultivated their prayer effectiveness through concentrated, focused worship. Joy Dawson, one of my personal mentors, is such an intercessor.

Joy, associated for years with Youth With A Mission (YWAM), is particularly known for her outstanding teaching on intercession, holiness and intimacy with God. I consider Joy's book *Intimate Friendship with God* a true classic. In my early years of developing an understanding of intercession, I would often spend entire days in my prayer closet just listening to one audiocassette after another of Joy's teachings. Later, I had the privilege of serving with Joy and her husband, Jim, for many years on America's National Prayer Committee.

It was during one of our all-day prayer retreats with the National Prayer Committee in Washington, D.C., that Joy uniquely demonstrated how to see God bigger. We were midway through a morning of seeking and waiting on God when Joy began to worship God audibly, praising a variety of aspects of His nature and character. As usual, Joy filled her worship with God's Word.

I learned by praying with Joy over the years that she had developed a lifelong habit of spending many early morning hours regularly saturating herself in the Scriptures. In so doing, she had compiled her own concordance of scores of Bible passages focusing on who God is and what He is like.

And it was not just head knowledge. Joy studied the Light! Her prayers were filled with God because she knew who He was, whereas my prayers too often seemed as if they were reflecting the light of an old, worn-out lantern. Joy's were much more like that of a Fresnel lens. Her praise reflected God brilliantly and beautifully.

That day the light was reflecting especially brightly as Joy worshiped. All of us felt as if we had been lifted into the presence of God as this precious worshiper filled her prayers with praises of God's nature and character. Repeatedly, Joy would speak that memorable phrase Jesus used in confronting Satan while fasting in the wilderness. It is a phrase Joy often uses when praying (see Luke 4:4,8,12). "It is written," Joy would declare, and then follow that phrase with a bold declaration from some Bible passage about who God is, what He is like, what He has done or what He will do for those who seek Him. I thought to myself, *God always gets bigger when Joy prays!* And that morning was no exception.

Suddenly, Joy did something rather startling. She stopped, mid-sentence, interrupting her praise. What Joy did in that moment I had never seen anyone do before. She spoke directly to the devil and abruptly declared, "Satan, I'm not the least bit impressed by you," and, with hardly a pause, continued on with seeing God even bigger through her worship.

Through years of saturating herself in an understanding of God's nature and character, Joy had come to understand this vital principle: *The bigger we see God through our worship, the smaller Satan becomes in his capacity to defeat us.* Further, the more we understand Satan's diminished capacity, the more powerful our prayers of intercession become. And worship makes all this happen, allowing us to expand and increase our knowledge of God, thus providing us with a path to much greater power in our praying.

PRAYING BIG PRAYERS

Sadly, it seems some believers almost negate—and certainly diminish—the potential of the power of their worship and intercession by their own faithless words spoken during prayer. We verbally lament over the many pressing problems and attacks of the enemy to the point that we almost lose faith—we can hardly believe that victory is even possible. Joy Dawson points out that this can be especially devastating to our prayers of intercession.

During that same worship and intercession retreat with the National Prayer Committee, Joy described being invited to participate in a time of prayer in Europe a few months earlier. A room full of young, would-be missionaries was waiting when Joy arrived. Soon, the prayer meeting was underway.

But it was not long before Joy realized there was a problem. Participants filled their prayers with too much of the negative. This "bad thing" and that "horrible circumstance" were the focuses of their praying. Nothing of God's greatness or power was voiced. There was little if any praise. This continued for more than half an hour.

> The bigger we see God, the bigger we pray. And the bigger we pray, the greater our answers.

Joy tried to be gracious but knew if she continued praying with these young people very long, her faith to intercede effectively would be seriously hindered. She stood up and graciously, though boldly, told the group, "I'm truly sorry, but I've been here only a short while, and it's already evident you're more impressed with the power of Satan than you are with the awesomeness of

God. So I need to ask if I may be excused!"

Joy was not being unkind, just responsive to the concerns of her heart that the unintentional nonfocus of their prayers that morning was making God smaller—at least in her eyes. To Joy, big prayers only happen through those who see God big. And that is why our third worship reality is so critical to this matter of intercessory worship. Worship, indeed, enlarges God, something you can easily apply daily:

> ### *Declare in song and prayer God's greatness in comparison to every attack of the enemy.*

The bigger we see God, the bigger we pray. And the bigger we pray, the greater our answers. To totally transform nations will take some pretty big prayers. To literally reach every family and person on Earth with the gospel, while discipling whole nations in the process, will take huge prayers.

So, let's not let the enemy make God small in our thinking, praying or planning! Worship God fervently. Worship Him passionately. Worship Him aggressively and extravagantly. You will soon *see* God big—and *pray* big prayers. Best of all, you will experience the joy of the Lord that the Bible says will make you strong (see Neh. 8:10). And that, beloved worshiper, leads us to our next key worship reality.

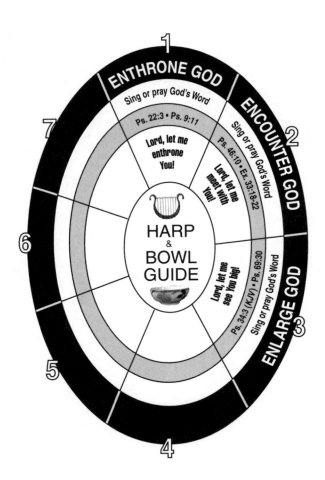

WORSHIP ENJOYS GOD
THE CLIFFS OF MOLOKAI

It was an early Sunday flight to the island of Kauai in Hawaii where I was to speak that morning. Hawaii is a favorite ministry destination for my wife, Dee, and me because of the beauty of just being there and for the opportunity to minister to believers hungry to see God display His glory throughout their islands.

When we had been in the air only a few minutes, the pilot of the small commuter plane commented that just off the lower left wing was the island of Molokai, population 7,000. The dim haze of an early dawn oozed through thick clouds hovering just above, creating a deep red-brown hue hanging over the island like a huge rust-colored blanket.

What a desolate place that has to be, I thought. Then I remembered that I once flew into Molokai in a private plane. At that time, a pastor from Honolulu where I was ministering had just acquired his pilot's license and wanted to fly somewhere. Molokai had a little-used airfield, so that was his choice. We flew there and back, landing quickly, stepping out of the plane to stretch and taking off again. I was not impressed. So brief was the experience that it was hardly an experience at all.

Now, 27 years later, gazing at Molokai from a distance, I realized I would be going there the following Sunday to speak at a local church. "Maybe I'll see the desolation close up," I said and chuckled to myself.

Over the years, Dee and I had made many trips to Hawaii, most often to spend times of ministry coupled with rest, and usually went to our favorite island, Maui. Often when staying on Maui's north shore, we would see Molokai across the Pacific, and experience that same sense of desolation. Molokai did not look inviting at all.

The locals on Molokai refer to their home as the forgotten island. For centuries other Hawaiians referred to it as the Dark Island. It was on Molokai that the famed Flemish priest Father Damien died of leprosy in the late 1880s. He was there to minister to the islanders, who were steeped in traditions of witchcraft and superstition.

In fact, Molokai was the island where all the powerful *kahuna* (priests) were trained in the ways of witchcraft. Some kahuna, tradition tells us, could "pray a person to death." They clearly understood the supernatural. Later I would learn that this island played host to the Kahuna school where sorcerers were trained and sent to other islands.[1] It truly was the Dark Island!

GETTING CLOSER: A JOURNEY OF JOY

The following Sunday, an interisland commuter plane took off again for Molokai from Maui's Kahului airport. Even close up my initial impression was the same—this was indeed a desolate island. But that began to change as Pastor Michael Zarle took me on a brief but interesting drive along Molokai's southwest coast.

Soon I was speaking to a small but lively group of worshipers who were keeping the incense of worship rising from this island.

I finished my ministry that morning and boarded the commuter departing for Maui. Then something remarkable happened. Immediately after takeoff, the pilot flew the small plane directly over the beautiful cliffs of Molokai. It's hard to describe the awe and wonder of looking straight down those sheer walls of beauty from less than a few hundred feet above. It was breathtaking. I cannot recall having seen such a beautiful sight in all the journeys my wife and I have taken around the world in the past 20 years of ministry. I wondered to myself how much of the grandeur and majesty of this island I had missed just because I had not come close enough to see its beauty. I had almost missed the view of a lifetime—and the pure joy this view afforded—because I had never come close enough. Getting closer changed everything!

Reflecting on the wonder of that moment, I could not help but think of those who genuinely know God, in Christ, but have not come close enough to really see Him in all His beauty. Worship, of course, is the key to bringing us close. It is a journey of joy that takes us closer and closer to the true beauty and wonder of God, revealing to us more fully the pure pleasure of His presence.

Madame Guyon, the seventeenth-century French mystic, pursued with an almost defiant passion an inner revelation of the fullness of God. Her quest, which landed her in prison at the hands of the ecclesiastical authorities of her day, led Guyon to remarkable insights regarding prayer. She discovered prayer to be, in its essence, experiencing the joy of who God is.

Tracing her own journey of prayer, and applying what she had learned to all such seekers, Guyon wrote, "In the beginning, you were led into His presence by prayer; but now, as prayer continues, the prayer actually *becomes* His presence."[2]

What an extraordinary truth! Guyon then amplified this thought by explaining how God's Spirit drives us onward toward this goal, adding, "The Spirit moves us forward, plunging us toward the ultimate end. And what is the ultimate end? It is union with God."[3]

The old Westminster Catechism defines this ultimate goal similarly: "The chief end of man is to glorify God and enjoy Him forever." This suggests that worship is more than merely a means to an end—it is the end itself. Further, this process of cultivating our ultimate end of union with

God before we actually achieve it has not only the capacity to transform nations as we pursue this goal, but also to provide us incredible joy as our journey unfolds.

The psalmist said it thus, "In Your presence is fullness of joy; at Your right hand are pleasures forevermore" (Ps. 16:11, *NKJV*). True, this verse may well picture the believer's ultimate end, our eternal ecstasy with God, but there is another truth revealed in this promise. Great joy is also to be found simply by entering into and waiting within God's presence, a thought that leads to our next worship reality: *Worship enjoys God.* Expanded to our fourth intercessory worship principle:

> ### *Worship provides a place of entry into the delights and pleasures of God's presence.*

Few have fascinated me as much in their passion to become a "God Chaser" (to borrow Tommy Tenney's term) as has Francis of Assisi, the son of a wealthy twelfth-century Italian merchant. Born Francesco de Pietro Bernardone, he made such a global impact through his life that, as stated earlier, generations now know him simply as Francis of Assisi.

What most marked Francis of Assisi's life was his passion for God. His pure enjoyment of God seems almost unmatched since the early apostles. Such was evident when he wrote to his brothers:

> We should wish for nothing else and have no other desire, we should find no pleasure or delight in anything except in our Creator, Redeemer, and Savior; He alone is true God, perfect, good, all good, every good, and the true and supreme good . . . loving and gentle, kind and understanding.[4]

In this same discourse Francis elaborated at length:

> Nothing, then, must keep us back, nothing separate us from him, nothing come between us and him. At all times and seasons, in every country and place, every day and all day, we must keep him in our hearts, where we must love, honor, adore, serve, praise and bless, glorify and acclaim, magnify and thank, the most high supreme and eternal God, three in one, Father, Son, and Holy Spirit, Creator of all and the Savior of those who believe in him, who hope in him, and who love him; with-

out beginning and without end, he is unchange-
able, invisible, indescribable and ineffable, incom-
prehensible, unfathomable, blessed and worthy of
all praise . . . lovable, delightful and utterly desir-
able beyond all else, for ever and ever.[5]

ABSOLUTE JOY

Francis of Assisi's life was clearly a journey of joy. It was a
life that impacted millions, including another worshiping intercessor, the seventeenth-century monk, Brother
Lawrence, who personified practicing God's presence.
He offered us this insight regarding man's ultimate goal:
"The thing we ought to purpose to ourselves in this life is to
become the most perfect worshipers of God we can possibly
be as we hope to be through all eternity."[6]

Both Francis and Lawrence understood that
approaching God through pure worship was to enter an
atmosphere of absolute joy! In so doing, their very lives
became powerfully intercessory in the sense that God
allowed them to intervene in the transformation of multitudes, even long after they were gone.

I want to particularly emphasize the total joy that
flooded all they did! It is a joy available to any believer who

pursues God in worship, because *worship enjoys God*. The psalmist described such worshipers: "What joy for those you choose to bring near, those who live in your holy courts. What joys await us inside your holy Temple" (Ps. 65:4, *NLT*).

Elsewhere we read, "How lovely is your dwelling place, O LORD Almighty. I long, yes, I faint with longing to enter the courts of the LORD. With my whole being, body and soul, I will shout joyfully to the living God. . . . How happy are those who can live in your house, always singing your praises" (Ps. 84:1-2,4, *NLT*). How many believers today have tasted such joy? Imagine the impact such joyful worshipers would have on those around them!

Tozer spoke of cultivating this joy and linked it to the fear of God when he wrote: "I believe that the reverential fear of God mixed with love and fascination and astonishment and admiration and devotion is the most enjoyable state and the most purifying emotion the human soul can know."[7]

Imagine a joy that transcends anything we could possibly anticipate or experience in our lifetimes. Picture it as beyond the joy of falling in love or the passion of marital intimacy. Think of it as surpassing the birthing of a child, wildly succeeding in a career, loving a grandchild or growing old in a happy marriage. Imagine all of that together but much, much more. Then, add to it total health with a complete absence of pain, fear, doubt and any form of discouragement. In other words, imagine a joy that is unimaginable. Imagine absolute joy.

Heaven holds just such joy, not because heaven happens to be heaven, but because God will be worshiped "close up" in heaven—and *worship enjoys God.*

DUMP TRUCKS IN HEAVEN

I recall a childhood experience from my third-grade Sunday School class. A classmate, Billy, had an argument with our teacher, Mrs. Schmidt. She had tried to lure Billy into praying the sinner's prayer by promising him that if he would but pray this simple prayer, he would go to heaven—*free of charge.* Billy would not comply. The fact was, Billy had a strange passion for dump trucks. He insisted that Mrs. Schmidt promise him there would be dump trucks in heaven or he would not go. (I recall he specifically demanded a red one!)

Mrs. Schmidt almost lost a convert trying to explain to Billy there would be no need for dump trucks in heaven, because we would have all-new bodies when we got there, with different desires. But she finally gave in and won Billy over by promising that God could do anything: If, when Billy got to heaven, he still felt the need for a red dump truck, God was certainly capable of making him one—on the spot.

I was sure Mrs. Schmidt was lying through her teeth, but I kept my mouth shut because she talked with God a lot during our class, as if she knew Him personally, and I did not want to get on her bad side. Plus, I was inwardly hoping there would be tractors in heaven—green ones—they were my third-grade fascination.

And herein lies the whole of the problem with our concept of heaven as well as with this entire matter of joy. We try to equate the beauty of heaven, and joy itself, with our human understanding or emotions. If we happen to be into dump trucks or tractors, then for heaven to be heaven there had better be some dump trucks and tractors.

Only a few weeks after Billy's dump-truck episode, an evangelist came to our small church in northern Wisconsin. Revival resulted—a true, heaven-sent visitation that lasted for more than eight weeks with services six nights a week. Several hundred found Christ and the church grew significantly.

But as an eight-year-old I struggled to understand why we had to go to church every night and especially why it was necessary to sing certain hymns and choruses so many times. One particular night, the meeting went rather long and I fell asleep in the pew. Suddenly, I awoke to the strains of "Amazing Grace," which I was certain they had been singing when I first fell asleep only minutes earlier. The hymn continued even longer, and it seemed as if the evangelist were making up new verses just to keep it going.

Then, as I lay there exhausted, longing to go home, I recall the preacher shouting, "Isn't this wonderful? This is exactly what heaven will be like!" Trying to go back to sleep, I recall thinking, *Oh, no, there's going to be church every night in heaven!*

THE BEAUTY REALM OF GOD

Even as an eight year old, I was already cultivating a misconception about eternity, and heaven in particular, thinking of it as a place rather than as a Person. True, it *will* be a place, a very real place, but heaven will only be what it is because of the presence of the Person of Christ, the Bridegroom, and the splendor of God's presence around His throne. Our joy will be in our worship, for *worship enjoys God!*

Mike Bickle captures this thought well when he speaks about "the beauty realm of God" that King David experienced in the Tabernacle of David. We, too, can catch glimpses of it even now, but will only experience it in totality when we spend eternity in God's presence. Bickle writes: "Feasting on the beauty realm of God was a primary desire of David—and one of the secrets of this quality of worship (see Psalm 27:4)."[8]

Bickle adds, "In fact, David was the first man to bring into one context worship singers, musicians and intercessors. I believe that many of the intercessory psalms were written on site in the Tabernacle of David."[9]

> I was cultivating a misconception about eternity, and heaven in particular, thinking of it as a place rather than as a Person.

This joy of worship surrounding David's Tabernacle is so important that I will devote a second book in my *Delight* trilogy, titled *Patterns of Delight*, to the theme of the Tabernacle of David. This is especially vital because Scripture clearly speaks of an ultimate restoration of

David's Tabernacle (see Acts 15:16-18) as being linked to a future massive harvest of all peoples. This text, to be revisited in depth in *Patterns of Delight*, quotes the apostle James, who was restating the ancient prophecy of Amos (see Amos 9:11-15). James declared:

> This conversion of Gentiles agrees with what the prophets predicted. For instance, it is written: "Afterward I will return, and I will restore the fallen kingdom [tent, *NIV*] of David. From the ruins I will rebuild it, and I will restore it, so that the rest of humanity might find the Lord, including the Gentiles" (Acts 15:15-17, *NLT*).

But here I want to primarily emphasize the "joy factor" that becomes so essential in powerful intercessory worship. Further discussing this theme, Mike Bickle refers to the rapidly growing harp and bowl movement, mentioned earlier, that draws its focus from the picture in Revelation 5:8-10 (described in chapter 1). It is here we see the living creatures and elders coming before God's throne with "harps" (symbolic of worship) and "bowls" (filled with prayers of intercession), releasing a new worship song of the redeemed who are saved out of every tribe, tongue, people and nation.

Intercession, of course, is a key to this ingathering; but as Mike Bickle contends, if joy does not saturate our intercession, it grows both weak and wearisome. He explains, "I believe the harp and bowl model of intercessory worship is key to the present worldwide prayer movement because it creates the 'joy in the House of Prayer' about which Isaiah prophesied (see Isaiah 56:7)."

Does God call us to wear ourselves down in wearisome prayer? Absolutely not, He invites us to joy! Employ your own harp and bowl daily! It's easy:

> **Declare in song and prayer your delight and joy in God for who He is and what He has done.**

Bickle adds, "Our intercessory prayer furnaces can burn longer and brighter when they are fueled by love songs to God. As music and praise from the beauty realm of God are joined with the prayers of the saints and offered at the throne of God, great spiritual benefits are released on earth."[10]

CATCHING A GLIMPSE

During the second day of my 40-day worship fast, I caught a small but significant glimpse of this "beauty realm of

God" and how its resulting joy helps fuel our "prayer furnaces." I had determined at God's direction on the previous day, that each of my daily prayer times for the following 40 days would consist entirely of worshiping the Lord in song—including the singing of all my prayers. However, I had no idea how these worship times would unfold, because I had never before attempted something like this over such a long period of time.

It was now the second day of my fast, and I realized I had a long way to go. I had decided to work at home that day on some ministry projects. At noon, I went into my prayer closet intending to spend that day's hour of my worship-fast alone, something I had done the day before with hundreds at the World Prayer Center. I was not exactly sure how it would go, but I knew this was to begin the pattern of many days of singing both my worship and prayers!

Of course, it was not that I had never spontaneously worshiped the Lord in song; but on the only other occasion that involved a prolonged time (an entire day), I had worshipped with other intercessors. But now I was to do it alone—and for 39 days! I turned off the prayer-closet light, so I would not be distracted by anything in the room—including maps of various countries as well as pictures of our Every Home for Christ staff and other Christian leaders and their families. I wanted to focus totally on the Lord.

Sitting on my comfortable cushions, I remember praying, "Lord, I'm not exactly sure how to do this, but here goes!" and I began to sing. I cannot recall the specific content of those first attempts at spontaneous song, but I vividly remember running out of steam in about 10 minutes. The words clearly made little sense, and the melody, I am sure, sounded pathetic. I started to chuckle in embarrassment, interrupting my song with a barely audible, "This is silly!"

Instantly, a voice within responded, *No, it's beautiful. Your singing blesses Me!*

I knew the Lord was speaking and so I continued, though with some degree of difficulty. I recalled the Bible promise a day earlier: "You satisfy me more than the richest of foods. I will praise you with songs of joy" (Ps. 63:5, *NLT*). I felt I was to continue no matter how uncreative or insignificant my song seemed. Besides, it was not for me; it was unto the Lord. He was hearing my heart, not my lips or my voice.

My goal was to spend at least an hour of worship in song. I decided not to look at my watch for fear of being discouraged if I could not complete an entire hour. The room was dark because the lights were out, so I could not see my watch anyway. Suddenly, it seemed as if the heavens above me opened.

A RAIN OF JOY

Moments after I decided to continue no matter what, God's glory came. It felt like a rain of joy. My song obviously did not end. For a time it seemed like it never would. Nor did I find myself growing weary.

What had begun with a sense of awkwardness now became an entry into the beauty realm of God. Finally, I stood to leave my prayer closet. As I opened the door, the light from the outside hall quickly blinded me. Once my eyes adjusted, I looked at my watch. I was stunned—what had seemed like only a few minutes had, in reality, been hours.

In that moment I grasped something of an understanding of the pure joy of God's presence when we observe nothing but glimpses of the unending facets of His beauty. This, I realized, could well be an eternal preoccupation. I had always thought of heaven as a place to do things that we enjoy on Earth, only with bodies absent of pain. I recall hearing clever sermons as a youth on how heaven would include such blessings as "fuzzless peaches and seedless watermelon" and where the average golf score for 18 holes always would be *exactly* 18. Now it was clearer than ever that the pure joy of heaven would be our enjoying more and more of the beauty of God.

A vital aspect of that joy, I realized, was the incredible delight of making it possible for millions of others from every tribe, tongue, people and nation to join with us in this joy. Worship, indeed, enjoys God and enjoys bringing others into that joy. What could possibly be more eternally exciting?

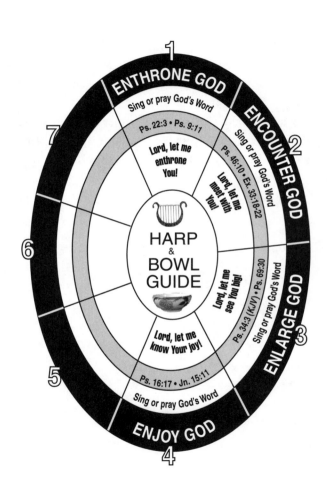

HARP
&
BOWL
GUIDE

1 — ENTHRONE GOD
Sing or pray God's Word
Ps. 22:3 • Ps. 9:11
Lord, let me enthrone You!

2 — ENCOUNTER GOD
Sing or pray God's Word
Ps. 46:10 • Ex. 33:18-22
Lord, let me meet with You!

3 — ENLARGE GOD
Sing or pray God's Word
Ps. 34:3 (KJV) • Ps. 69:30
Lord, let me see You big!

4 — ENJOY GOD
Sing or pray God's Word
Ps. 16:17 • Jn. 15:11
Lord, let me know Your joy!

WORSHIP ENLISTS GOD

FIRE FROM HEAVEN

"Whenever the church has come out of her lethargy, rising from her sleep and into the tides of revival and spiritual renewal, always the worshipers were back of it."[1] These words of A. W. Tozer bring us to yet another vital worship reality: *Worship enlists God.*

Revival, true revival, is always the heart's cry of any committed believer. And central to every revival is worship.

In fact, it was Tozer who specifically defined revival in terms of worship. He emphasized:

> In my study and observations, a revival generally results in a sudden bestowment of a spirit of worship. This is not the result of engineering or manipulation. It is something God bestows on people hungering and thirsting for him. With this spiritual renewing will come a blessed spirit of loving worship.2

Worship, then, not only helps bring revival and sustains it but also opens the heavens for more of God so that worship, and the revival itself, can expand further. This results in the release of an even greater increase of our awareness of God, which is the essence of revival.

Additionally, intercessory worship releases something of God's glory into circumstances that otherwise would seem hopeless. When this involves worship-saturated intercession, it means we are intervening in the needs of others (intercession) by enlisting the fullness of God to assist us (worship), thus engaging in intercessory worship. Summed up as our fifth intercessory worship principle:

Worship provides our primary means to mobilize and release the resources of God into the needs of peoples and nations.

One thing is certain, transforming peoples and nations through a full revelation of Jesus Christ, accomplished by literally reaching all of these peoples specifically and individually with the gospel, will require a miracle. Of course, only God can perform true miracles. Thus, we need to include the God of the miraculous in all of our plans and strategies if we hope to accomplish our objective. Intercessory worship is the only means I can conceive of that would help Christ's Body achieve this goal.

How do we tap this power? It is worship that *enlists* God and intercession that *involves* God, together resulting in a release of the spiritual and material resources needed to touch and transform individuals and nations. The psalmist worshipfully pictured the power we need when he sang, "You are the God who performs miracles; you display your power among the peoples" (Ps. 77:14). We worship in the same manner as David when we do this important act of worship:

Declare in song and prayer that God's power is being released into your needs and into the nations.

All of this, of course, involves spiritual warfare. But our warfare is victorious only if God is in it. Worship, by enlisting God, assures us that He will be in it.

A WINDOW FOR GOD'S GLORY

Tommy Tenney, in his book *God's Favorite House*, explains, "There is no better way to wage spiritual warfare than to turn on the light of God's glory by ushering in His manifest presence."[3] Tenney adds, "When the heavens are open and God's light shines on the darkness, every demon and dark work is forced out because the gates of hell can never prevail or even put up a respectable fight when the very presence of the King of glory shows up."[4]

Regarding this call to worship and its resulting impact on a great harvest of lost people coming to Christ, Tenney concludes, *The hungry will find you!* They will follow the 'light' to its source, just as the wise men of old followed the heavenly light to Christ. Worship opens a window—a window for God's glory to stream down. Humanity is then drawn to the light."[5]

In both the Old and New Testaments we see evidence of this reality that *worship enlists God*. We recall the familiar account of King Jehoshaphat and the people of Judah facing the humanly insurmountable enemies of Moab and Ammon (see 2 Chron. 20:1-28). A great multitude of God's people had gathered in a vast multitude to fast and pray, crying out to God for victory. As they humbled themselves before the Lord, the prophet Jahaziel stood in their midst, prophesying, "March down against them. . . . You will not have to fight this battle. Take up your positions; stand firm and see the deliverance the LORD will give you . . . Do not be afraid; do not be discouraged" (vv. 16-17).

It seems this prophecy was somewhat confusing to both the king and his commanders. Why does an army "march down against them" and "take up your positions," which suggest movement, then "stand firm" and "not have to fight," which clearly suggest doing nothing? This probably led to some degree of discussion, because the Bible relates, "After consulting the people, Jehoshaphat appointed men to sing to the LORD and to praise Him . . . as they went out at the head of the army" (v. 21).

Notice, in particular, the comment "after consulting the people." It is clear that something prompted this consultation. Could it be that Jehoshaphat said to his captains and commanders, "God has told us to stand still because the victory is His, but He's also told us to move into position! Any suggestions?" I can imagine someone responding,

"Perhaps, O King, our position ought to be that of worship, because God says He will come to dwell amid those who praise Him!"

We do know that worship was the strategy chosen because of what happens next. The passage continues, "As they began to sing and praise, the LORD set ambushes against the men of Ammon and Moab and Mount Seir . . . and they were defeated" (v. 22). So massive was the victory that it required three full days to gather up all the spoils. Worship, clearly, had enlisted God.

A similar worship victory can be found in the experience of Paul and Silas while incarcerated at Philippi. It was a life-threatening situation, but a miracle happened. The Bible says, "Suddenly there was such a violent earthquake that the foundations of the prison were shaken. At once all the prison doors flew open" (Acts 16:26).

Interestingly, this miracle resulted *during* a worship encounter. When the earthquake occurred, Paul and Silas were both singing hymns and offering praise. Again, worship had enlisted God.

A FALLING WALL

A memorable journey my wife and I took with a small team of intercessors to the Buddhist land of Bhutan significantly amplified this worship reality. I had been invited to speak at a conference of some 1,500 leaders from throughout the Himalayas who were meeting in Darjeeling, India. Our original plans for the journey included a visit first to Nepal for an Every Home for Christ leadership meeting for South Asia, followed by traveling directly to Darjeeling for the conference. But as my wife and I were making travel plans and looking at a map, I noticed, quite by accident, how very close our trip would take us to the tiny nation of Bhutan. For several years I had

> I felt God was calling me to go to the Berlin Wall and physically lay my hands on the wall, commanding it to come down in Jesus' name.

felt a burden to go to this closed Buddhist land to pray that it would be opened to the gospel. In late 1987 I had felt a similar burden regarding East Germany and the Berlin Wall.

As I told in my book *The Jericho Hour*, God had deeply burdened me in a late-night prayer encounter in November 1987 to confront the strongholds of communism in

Eastern Europe. Immediately I saw in my mind the Berlin Wall as the primary symbolic stronghold of the region.

More specifically, I felt God was calling me to go to the Berlin Wall and physically lay my hands on the wall, commanding it to come down, "in Jesus' name." Interestingly, the total prayer assignment for the entire journey was to consist of a mere five words—"In Jesus' name come down!"

As I wrote in *The Jericho Hour*, the journey finally took place (after a month of prayer) in January 1988, and the five-word prayer became a reality. The following year the wall came down, and Every Home for Christ saw immediate results. In less than six months after the wall fell, our West German EHC office received more than 120,000 requests from East Berlin and surrounding areas for Bible lessons about Jesus.

In the decade following, home-to-home literature campaigns were conducted in all Eastern European countries as well as throughout Russia and the former Soviet republics, touching some 40 million households in this greater Eurasia region.

Of course, I realized my prayers alone did not make all this happen, but I certainly felt a small part of the miracle. Later I would hear a remarkable account of how, eight days before the first bulldozer actually broke through the Berlin Wall, a group of teenage worshipers from a West Berlin church had climbed up on the wall and were singing choruses. West German soldiers were about to remove them when one of their officers said, "They're only singing songs about God, leave them be."

When the first bulldozer arrived eight days later to break the first opening into the wall, it hit the same spot where the youth had been singing. I have often wondered, though I cannot confirm it, if that was the same spot where I placed my hands when praying my five-word prayer. I would not be surprised if it was!

FIRE AND THE DRAGON

Realizing how very close we would be to the border of Bhutan as we traveled to Darjeeling, I had a strange sense that this tiny "Dragon Kingdom" (the name given it by the people of Bhutan) would prove key to the ultimate evangelization and even transformation of all of the Himalayan nations, including those of China, Tibet, Nepal, India, Pakistan and even deeply troubled Afghanistan.

I contacted our director in Nepal to see if we would have enough time to travel to Bhutan—even if our visit was only an hour long. At least that would allow a few moments for prayer.

Our director's response promptly followed, explaining that if we traveled an entire day by Jeep from the border of Nepal when our EHC meetings ended, we could reach Bhutan late that same evening and spend at least one night there. But the following morning it would be necessary to depart early for Darjeeling.

I also asked about getting visas for Bhutan and received more encouraging news. Normally such visas take months to obtain. But our director explained that an international town on the border of India and Bhutan, named Phuntsholing, required no visa. Because the two national borders of Bhutan and India meet on Main Street, a free flow of traffic was permitted back and forth at this particular point.

Bhutan's main border, with much more restrictive customs and immigration, is some 25 miles farther into the nation. So, praise God, no visas would be required to plant our feet on the soil of the Dragon Kingdom.

Following a grueling nine-hour journey from Nepal's eastern border, we finally arrived in Phuntsholing, Bhutan, late on a warm and misty Sunday night. It was April 19, 1998.

The first building we saw in Phuntsholing was an ornate Buddhist temple and monastery. We knew immediately this was to be the focal point for prayer later that evening. We quickly located a hotel that had exactly the number of rooms we needed for our small team, and we dropped off our luggage so we could return to the temple.

We paired up and quietly began walking around the temple, declaring our prayers and praises over this tiny Dragon Kingdom of Bhutan—hardly a speck on a map, with a population considerably less than a million. Yet I felt once again that Bhutan was somehow a key in God's plans for all of the Himalayas and that we were there as part of His plan.

Even the fact that Bhutan is known as the Dragon Kingdom seemed significant. It reminded me that we were confronting the Prince of Darkness, who is referred to in Scripture as "the great dragon" (Rev. 12:9).

The youngest member of our team, Mike Clinton, prayed an especially interesting prayer that night. He asked God to send fire from heaven to burn away the scales from the eyes of those who were bound in spiritual darkness by the spirit of Tibetan Buddhism. Mike could not recall what prompted those specific words, but they soon proved prophetic.

We returned to our rooms late that evening and woke early enough the following morning to return to the temple for another season of prayer. This time we circled the temple seven times in intercessory worship.

Interestingly, Buddhist priests and devout Buddhist worshipers also were prayer walking around the temple. But their prayer walks included the spinning of small cylindrical prayer wheels that looked like colorfully painted, oversized tin cans. These were adorned with perhaps hundreds of hand-painted prayers to their demonic gods.

In addition there were perhaps 20 such prayer wheels on each of the four walls of this beautifully decorated temple. One wall consisted of a short staircase leading to a portion of the temple that included two huge cylinders the size of giant oil drums, again colorfully decorated with prayers to their demonic gods. These also could be rotated, but required considerably more effort.

CONFRONTING THE COMPETITION

Tibetan Buddhists believe that each time a wheel is spun, it sends these printed prayers into the heavenlies and to their gods. But now, even as these Buddhist devotees were circling their temple time after time, we also were prayer walking. But our worship was intercessory worship. We were confronting the competition by enlisting God through our prayers and praises for all the people of the Himalayas.

Just before our departure from the temple, I climbed the stairs to the huge drums and placed my hands on them, just as I had done at the Berlin Wall a decade earlier. I was keenly aware that something significant was happening in the heavenlies.

We departed Bhutan on schedule and traveled throughout the day over the treacherous one-lane roads heading up through the Himalayan foothills toward the mountain town of Darjeeling. More than once I put my head out the window of our Jeep and literally looked straight down more than a mile and a half into the valley below. This was not too difficult to do as my side of the Jeep was actually hovering near the edge! I am sure we all learned some new ways to pray during that eight-hour journey up the mountain.

The conference in Darjeeling was inspiring and significant. Led by Thomas Wang, one of the founders of the AD 2000 and Beyond Movement, the gathering brought together more than 1,500 leaders representing 52 ministry strategies and organizations with a burden to evangelize the Himalayas. Our gathering was known as HIMCOWE—Himalayan Congress on World Evangelization.

I represented Every Home for Christ's specific contribution to the goals of the conference. Our part included working with several of these groups to take the gospel, in print or audio form, to every home in every village throughout the Himalayas. I also addressed the gathering on the role of prayer in completing the Great Commission.

It seemed unusually significant that the Lord sent us by way of Bhutan to declare His glory over this dark region *before* bringing us to Darjeeling to discuss ways to transform the Himalayas through the gospel. I had little idea, however, of how truly significant that brief Bhutan encounter would prove to be.

THE FIRE FALLS

Dee and I left Darjeeling for New Delhi, India, where we had planned to set aside a few days for rest before heading to Europe for additional meetings. We especially looked forward to our first visit to the famed Taj Mahal, just a few hours' drive from India's capital of New Delhi.

Arriving at our hotel in New Delhi, I quickly purchased copies of the *International Herald Tribune*, anxious to see what news I had missed in the previous two weeks. Not only did I purchase the English edition for that particular day, but the bookshop had two older issues from the previous week. So, being something of a "news nut" (to quote my wife), I purchased all three, but I only read that day's copy, setting aside the other two, intending to read them later.

After getting some much-needed rest and taking a day trip to the Taj Mahal, it was time to leave for Europe. We were hastily packing to head for the airport when I noticed the two unread newspapers, now more than a week old. I bent over to drop them into the wastebasket—and stopped abruptly.

I felt a strange impression, in the form of a question, *What if something important happened during those days that I was without a newspaper, and I missed it?*

I paused momentarily above the trash basket and opened one of the folded papers. It was the older of the two unread editions, from Thursday of the previous week. My eyes instantly focused on a headline that leaped from the page. It read: "Fire Destroys a Famed Buddhist Shrine in Bhutan." I could hardly believe my eyes. Had not one of our team members actually prayed for fire to come down?

The paper certainly captured my attention. The article began: "The Takstang Monastery in Bhutan, one of the oldest and best-known shrines in the Himalayan Buddhist world outside of Tibet, was destroyed by fire Sunday night, Bhutanese officials have announced."

It was the very night, April 19, that we had prayed around another temple monastery not far away, the one at the Bhutanese border town of Phuntsholing. That was where Mike Clinton had prayed for fire to fall from heaven. He had specifically asked God to send His fire to burn away the scales from the eyes of those blinded by the darkness of Tibetan Buddhism.

But little did I know how significant the Takstang monastery was to the practice of Buddhism throughout all the Himalayas.

A DISAPPEARING DRAGON

The Takstang temple monastery was built centuries ago on the face of a 2,500-foot cliff high above the road from Paro in Bhutan on the Tibetan border near Mount Chomo Lhari. This monastery had existed in Bhutan since at least the ninth century.

According to the region's mythology, a famous Buddhist saint from India, Guru Rimpoche, is said to have landed here on the back of a flying tiger in the eighth century, miraculously bringing Buddhism into the Himalayas from the plains of India. The word *Takstang*, meaning "tiger's den," is derived from this belief that the flying tiger landed there bringing Guru Rimpoche. From here, Buddhist historians believe that Rimpoche's teachings spread to Tibet, perhaps on that very road from Paro to Mount Chomo Lhari. In other words, this temple was no ordinary temple. It is thought to be the primary point of entry of the spirit of Buddhism into *all* of the Himalayas, and particularly Tibet, the seat of Tibetan Buddhism.

The *Tribune* article concluded by quoting Kinley Dorji, editor of *Kuensel*, Bhutan's only newspaper, who had been to the Takstang Mountain on the Tuesday following the Sunday-night fire. He described the monastery as "totally gone."[6]

Within days of the Takstang fire, a team of Every Home for Christ workers began ministering in the mountainous regions of Tibet near the border of Nepal. In the very first villages visited, two Buddhists openly responded to the gospel and received Christ. Two days later, in a nearby village, two Buddhist priests, one the head of the local monastery, heard the gospel and also believed.

Then, following a nonstop, 14-hour trek at 17,000 feet, those same Christian workers came to a small village. In this single town, 70 villagers listened to the gospel and 4 made a public decision to accept Christ as Savior. The workers were later told that several others had received Christ but were afraid to declare it publicly.

The scales, indeed, seemed to be coming off the eyes of those blinded by Buddhism. One year later I picked up a copy of the *Denver Post* and read an article that further convinced me that our prayers had had a continuing effect. Once again the headline grabbed my attention, "Bhutan's Monarch Embraces Democracy, Himalayan Style." The article began, "King Jigme Singye Wangchuck, leader of the Himalayas' last Buddhist monarchy, boasts four wives, a passion for basketball and a gilded throne. His latest infatuation is democracy."[7]

After explaining how the king enjoys watching NBA basketball by satellite television, the article continued, "In a series of dramatic moves, the king has charted a course aimed at preparing this fabled land of myth and magic for the tedious realities of self-rule."

Realizing that our intercessory worship experience in Bhutan had been exactly one year earlier, I was especially stirred by the next statement:

Since last year, the ruler of the Thunder Dragon People has fired his top advisers, surrendered day-to-day control of his government, and, most important, given a group of long-time yes-men the right to throw him off his own throne.[8]

Could there be a correlation between that intercessory worship encounter at Phuntsholing the previous year and the "since last year" of the newspaper article? Even more recently, while at a missions conference in Australia, I decided to share the story of my team's worship experience in Bhutan. To my amazement, even before I was able to share my news, the host church's missions pastor presented a report of the congregation's past 12 months of missionary outreach—including a testimony about the miraculous planting of 14 New Testament fellowships within Bhutan in just the previous year.

Could it be that we are seeing the beginnings of a disappearing dragon in Bhutan? Is Satan, "the great dragon" (Rev. 12:9), starting to lose his grip on this tiny yet strategic stronghold called Bhutan? And could it mean the burning away of the scales from the eyes of multitudes of nonbelievers in all the Himalayas?

One thing is certain: worship, when linked to inter-cession, does indeed enlist God. And enlisting God is clearly essential to the transformation of nations through the gospel of Jesus Christ. Imagine how all this must excite the heart of God!

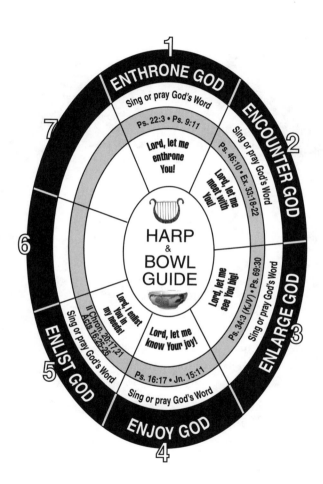

WORSHIP
EXCITES GOD
A DANCE OF DELIGHT

A chill had settled over the small wooded area near central Washington, D.C., where I had sat beside a huge rock, somewhat uncomfortably, praising the Lord audibly for eight hours. Several years earlier, while reading the writings of A. W. Tozer and others on worship, I had felt an urge to someday set aside an entire day just to praise God, from sunrise to sunset—audibly. I wanted to see what would happen if the only words I spoke for an entire day consisted of praise.

Now that day had arrived and most of it had passed. The goal of continuous, audible praise had been moderately achieved. By 4:30 in the afternoon my voice was getting weary, and the wooded area I had discovered at 7:30 A.M. (where I knew I could be secluded for the entire day) was getting cool as the sun was setting.

Little could I have known that I was about to be introduced, firsthand, to what I would later see as one of the most significant of these worship realities: *Worship excites God*. This reality is more fully described in a simple 14-word intercessory worship principle:

Worship provides the only true position from which we might bring God pure pleasure.

THE WARMTH OF WORSHIP

Then, in 1984, I traveled to Washington, D.C., for America's National Day of Prayer, scheduled for the first Thursday in May. I was in the D.C. area the previous Sunday to speak at the Church of the Apostles, an Episcopal church where our Change the World School of Prayer was scheduled for the following Saturday.

> I had sat in praise, stood in praise, knelt in praise and even walked the clearing several times in praise. What else could I do?

As I was preparing for the activities of that week, I realized Tuesday was free of all meetings. Nothing was on my schedule. No luncheon, dinner or appointments were scheduled for the day. I knew it would be the perfect occasion to fulfill my dream of a day of praise.

When Tuesday arrived, I arose early with my list of praise Scriptures in hand and set out to find a quiet place somewhere near our nation's capitol to spend the day in praise.

Driving along the George Washington Parkway, I saw a large wooded area not too far from the center of the city. I parked my car beside the road and, with my Bible and praise list, headed into the woods. I was encouraged when I found a small clearing, quite secluded, with a huge rock where I knew I could sit and praise the Lord for the rest of the day.

Sitting by that large stone in those woods near our Capitol, and praising the Lord for a whole day was the culmination of a desire that God had been stirring in my heart. I had for some time felt an inner longing to experience a full day of praise—aloud. I knew it was not to be a day of meditation, contemplation nor quiet Bible reading. It was to be a day of nothing but praise. I had even begun compiling numerous pages of praise Scriptures to help me fulfill this dream if and when this day came.

Now it was almost five o'clock in the evening and a heavy chill had settled in. As I looked toward the center of the clearing, a ray of sunlight streaked its way through the thick trees and that part of the clearing looked a bit warmer. So I stood and walked toward the warmth. But more than anything, I wanted to experience the warmth of God's presence through my worship.

By now my voice had grown hoarse and weak from this day of praise. I was running out of expressions of praise. I had praised God using every Scripture on my list at least twice. I was also running out of praise postures, though I am sure this did not matter to God. I had *sat* in praise, *stood* in praise, *knelt* in praise and even *walked* the clearing several times in praise. *What else can I do?* was a thought that crossed my mind.

MAKING GOD HAPPY

As I stood in the clearing, trying to catch the sun for a little warmth, I inwardly longed to reach up and touch God. This desire that seized me is hard to express in words. On the one hand, I wanted to feel God; but, on the other, I merely desired to please Him.

Then a rather unusual thought came to my mind. I longed to do something I had never done before in worship, public or private. I looked toward the top of the clearing and said, "Lord, there is one act of worship I've seen often in Scripture but have never done." I added, "Lord, I know King David did it and You said he was a man after Your own heart."

Oddly, I felt as if I needed to explain all this to God, as if He had no idea what I was thinking. So I continued, "Father, David danced before You with all his might, and I know this is something I've never done."

Somewhat ashamed, I added, "In fact, You know I've often considered people who do stuff like this overly emotional or even strange. And besides, I'm not even sure I know how to do it right."

My explanation was really more to myself than it was to God, and so I continued: "Lord, I do know the Hebrew word for dance means to 'whirl about,' so I guess that's what I'm supposed to do." Tearfully I added, "Lord, I'm just running out of words to praise You, so I think I'll just whirl about for a few minutes. Here goes!"

What happened next was totally unplanned on my part, and it was probably humorous to God. I started moving my feet up and down as I spun about. Then I started hopping. Soon I was whirling, hopping and spinning—with a periodic awkward leap thrown in for good measure. At one point I honestly thought I might hurt myself. Plus, I was quickly running out of breath.

The entire experience had lasted probably only 7 to 10 minutes when I started to laugh. To me, it was hilarious. I was sure that if a passerby had seen me they would have thought I was a lunatic. Yet, I continued both dancing and laughing. Then, I stopped and looked up, asking, "God, is this right?"

I really wondered if what I was doing mattered. What I felt next I will never forget—and it moved me immediately to tears. I knew God was speaking as I heard, *You'll never know the joy you're giving Me. You delight Me with your dance.*

I fell to my knees in that clearing, weeping. Nothing could have meant more to me than the sense that my worship had excited the heart of God. Indeed, in spite of those theologians who explain that God does not actually need our worship, I knew I was making God happy. Worship, I now understood, truly excites God. It is the only thing that really brings Him pure pleasure.

A SACRIFICE OF DELIGHT

Until now, each of our worship realities has focused primarily on the impact worship has on *us*—our personal and spiritual warfare, as well as our mission in life. Here we examine how our worship brings delight to the heart of our Lord.

Notice these words of the psalmist as he describes the focus of God's delight: "Praise his name with dancing, accompanied by tambourine and harp. For the LORD delights in his people; he crowns the humble with salvation" (Ps. 149:3-4, *NLT*).

Here God's delight in His people is described in the context of their worship. Further, this theme is linked to spiritual warfare as it impacts the nations. The psalm continues: "Let the praises of God be in their mouths, and a sharp sword in their hands—to execute vengeance on the nations . . ." (Ps. 149:6-7, *NLT*). Once again, as in numerous other places in the psalms, praise and worship are described in a context of touching all the earth, which is surely a reason praise so delights the heart of God (see Pss. 66:1-4,8; 67; 96:1-3,7-10; 98:1-4).

Generations later, the author of the book of Hebrews would show us more clearly why praise delights God. He wrote: "Through Jesus, therefore, let us continually offer to God a sacrifice of praise—the fruit of lips that confess his name" (Heb. 13:15). *Praise-filled worship is a sacrifice.* Hebrews 13:15 makes this clear. It is choice fruit offered to God. Thus, worship becomes the one true sacrifice that we can give God that truly brings Him delight. And it's simple to apply daily:

> *Declare in song and prayer your*
> *desire to excite the Lord through your*
> *worship and obedience.*

Of course, God clearly has all He needs within Himself and, in that sense, needs nothing. However, we also recognize He had a reason for creating humankind. Indeed, the powerful picture of praise around God's throne in

Revelation chapter 4 concludes with the living creatures and elders prostrating themselves, declaring: "'You are worthy, our Lord and God, to receive glory and honor and power, for you created all things, and by your will they were created and have their being'" (Rev. 4:11). The *New Living Translation* reads: "'You created everything, and it is *for your pleasure* that they exist and were created'" (emphasis added).

It is obvious, here, that all creation exists for God's pleasure, which naturally suggests there is something special about God's purpose in creating humankind. Of all creation, only human beings have the capacity to reason and understand what praise and adoration is all about. In addition, we have been given the ability to sing this adoration as well as to see and to comprehend the beauty of creation.

Animals might show forth God's beauty by their very existence, or, as in the case of the birds, glorify God through their song, but they don't have the gift of reason to recognize what they are actually doing. Neither can they comprehend the true beauty of what they see with their eyes.

A. W. Tozer believed that God made the flowers and the birds, and, indeed, all the wonders of creation simply so that we might delight in Him. This wise worshiper explained that any ordinary believer could tell you that God created those flowers to be beautiful and the birds to sing so that we might enjoy them. Scientists, however, will suggest that a male bird sings primarily to attract the female so they might nest and procreate—it is really all just instinctively biological. Tozer responds with this conclusion:

> It is at this point that I ask the scientist, "Why doesn't the bird just squeak and groan or gurgle? Why does he have to sing and warble and harmonize as though he had been tuned to a harp?" I think the answer is plain—it is because God made him to sing. If I were a male bird and wanted to attract a female I could turn handsprings or do any number of tricks. But why does the bird sing so beautifully? It is because the God who made him is the Chief Musician of the universe. He is the Composer of the cosmos. He made the harp in those little throats and the feathers around them and said, "Go and sing."[1]

Singing is God's idea!

HEAVENLY MUSIC

What about God Himself? Does He only enjoy listening to music, or does He make music? One of the most fascinating passages of Scripture concerning God's delight over His people is found in Zephaniah. Here the prophet records, "For the LORD Your God has arrived to live among you. He is a mighty savior. He will rejoice over you with great gladness. With his love, he will calm all your fears. He will exult over you by singing a happy song" (Zeph. 3:17, *NLT*). The *New International Version* translates that last phrase: "He will take great delight in you, he will quiet you with his love, he will rejoice over you with singing."

I recall a most unusual worship encounter that happened to a teenager named Joe in our youth group. Dee and I were ministering to young people in Sacramento, California, at the time. For about two years we had conducted periodic weekend prayer retreats, taking teenagers up into the Sierra Nevada mountains of Northern California. It was at the time that the Jesus Movement broke out, in 1969-1970.

Some estimates indicate more than 800,000 young people came to Christ in about a year and a half during those days. I have always been convinced that the passionate prayers of those teenagers in the mountains—as many as 180 youth at a single prayer retreat—helped pray this awakening into existence.

Joe attended one of these retreats and related a most unusual experience that resulted from a time of quiet worship. The format of the usual retreat, which was held from Friday evening to Saturday night or Sunday morning, included an entire night of prayer on Friday night, followed by several hours of quiet dialogue with God on Saturday morning.

During these quiet hours, each teenager would pray alone. Then, on Saturday afternoon, two or three hours were set aside for the young people to describe what they had experienced during their season of silence.

The teens were not permitted to talk to each other or communicate in any manner during quiet dialogue. Generally, it was to be a time of silent listening, meditation and being alone with God to love and worship Him.

At Joe's retreat that weekend, there had been an unusual sense of God's presence all through Friday night and into the early morning hours of Saturday. Teens were still weeping, worshiping and interceding over open Bibles as dawn slowly brightened the beautiful peaks of the tall Sierras rising above the camp.

As was customary, quiet dialogue began about nine o'clock Saturday morning. Amazing for a retreat of all teens, there was total silence as scores of young people, clutching Bibles and notepads, headed, without a whisper, out into the tall ponderosa pines and scrub oak covering the Sierra foothills.

When they returned three hours later, we spent most of that afternoon listening to all their testimonies as tearful teens described amazing encounters in God's Word, in worship and just in silent listening.

A DUET WITH HEAVEN

But it was Joe's experience that day that I will never forget. His eyes were red from weeping as he entered the lodge, and one could tell by the look on his face that something remarkable had happened. As other youths began sharing their experiences, Joe sat silent. I wondered if he would speak at all.

Later I learned Joe was hesitant because he could not find the words to describe what had happened to him. Even more, Joe was afraid others might not believe him. Finally, courage came and the young man spoke.

His voice faltering, Joe described how he found a quiet place deep among the tall trees and sat on an old, dead stump.

"I sat there for the longest time, not saying a word,"

Joe explained, adding as he looked toward me, "just as you told us!"

He slowly continued. "But it didn't work. All I heard was the wind blowing through the trees. I tried to hear God's voice, but I wasn't sure how to listen."

Joe's voice broke again as he continued. "Then, I decided just to sing my own song to the Lord. You said we could do that. So, I closed my eyes and sang. I made it up as I went along. And that's when something really weird happened."

I could tell Joe was hesitant, but he continued. "I heard footsteps come up behind me, and I turned to see who it was. But no one was there. I was really scared because even as I looked I could still hear the footsteps."

Joe cleared his throat and explained, "The sound of the footsteps stopped, like right beside me, but I just thought it was my imagination. So I closed my eyes and continued to sing."

The youth chuckled briefly, shaking his head as if to question what he knew had indeed happened. Then, he added, "I swear this is true. I felt a hand touch my right shoulder, and I heard another voice begin to sing."

No wonder Joe was reluctant to share. But there was more.

"Honestly," Joe explained, "I heard another voice singing, even though no one was there. But what blew me away was this voice was singing my own song—right with me, every word. Except the voice was singing in harmony. It was awesome."

Other teens were weeping as Joe shared, because they knew Joe. He was not one to exaggerate nor was he excessively emotional. In fact, Joe was more the typical youth-group skeptic, the type of teen whom youth leaders consider a doubting Thomas. That this happened to Joe held special significance.

To me, Joe's was something of a Zephaniah encounter that day. Somehow he had sung a duet with heaven. I cannot fully explain it, but I do know God delights in us and even sings over us. Remember Zephaniah's words: "He will exult over you by singing a happy song" (Zeph. 3:17, *NLT*). In Joe's case, it seems that God sang that song right along *with* him!

GOD'S HEART FOR GOD

Compare Zephaniah 3:17 with Revelation 4:11, where we are told that everything God has created is for His "pleasure" (*KJV, NLT*). God clearly delights in His children and actually seems to be especially delighted as we worship Him.

In fact, it appears that God delights in Himself in delighting in us even as we are delighting in Him—something you may want to think about for a moment before reading on!

Author John Piper helps tie all this together and links it powerfully to fulfilling the Great Commission in his provocative book *Let the Nations Be Glad*. Piper writes:

> The most passionate heart for God in all the universe is God's heart. This truth, more than any other I know, seals the conviction that worship is the fuel and goal of missions. The deepest reason why our passion for God should fuel missions is that God's passion for God fuels missions. Missions is the overflow of our delight in God because missions is the overflow of God's delight in being God. And the deepest reason why worship is the *goal* in missions is that worship is God's goal. We are confirmed in this goal by the Biblical record of God's relentless pursuit of praise among the nations. "Praise the Lord, all nations! Extol him, all peoples!" (Ps. 117:1). If it is God's goal it must be our goal.[2]

No doubt God's delight in our worship is precisely such because worship ultimately will establish His purpose for all of humankind—that the earth will be filled with the knowledge of the glory of the Lord "as the waters cover the sea" (Isa. 11:9; Hab. 2:14). In other words, worship leads to even more and greater worship.

John Piper further addresses the theological challenge of God's passion for Himself in seemingly requiring our worship, something that over the centuries has caused some to wonder if God is a bit egotistical in His passionate quest for worship. Concerning this enigma, Piper points us again to the old Westminster Catechism mentioned earlier. Piper says:

> What I am claiming is that the answer to the first question of the Westminster Catechism is the same when asked concerning God as it is when asked concerning man. Question: "What is the chief end of man?" Answer: "The chief end of man is to glorify God and enjoy him forever." Question: "What is the chief end of God?" Answer: "The chief end of God is to glorify God and enjoy himself forever."[3]

Piper expands on this thought by explaining the impact the Puritan revivalist Jonathan Edwards had on his own thinking. Piper explains:

God's passion for God is unmistakable. God struck me with this most powerfully when I first read Jonathan Edward's book entitled *The Dissertation Concerning the End for Which God Created the World.* There he piles reason upon reason and scripture on scripture to show this truth: "The great end of God's works, which is so variously expressed in Scripture, is indeed but ONE; and this *one* end is most properly and comprehensively called, THE GLORY OF GOD." In other words, the chief end of God is to glorify God, and enjoy himself for ever.[4]

IGNITING THE FLAME

All of this serves to strengthen the reality that *worship excites God*. It excites God because God is excited with Himself and knows that humankind can only experience His ultimate excitement *in Him*. It is that simple! And that is precisely why intercessory worship is so important in carrying out God's plans.

Someday, indeed, the smoke of the incense of worship from every village on Earth, even from every dwelling, will rise in adoration to our heavenly Father. As John Piper dreams, "When the flame of worship burns with the heat of God's true worth, the light of missions will shine to the most remote peoples on earth."[5]

God's true worth, then, ought to ignite within us a flame of such fervent intercessory worship that we are overwhelmed with a new zeal to touch and transform our families, neighbors and nations.

Toward this end may we risk something of our "religious" dignity in a humble attempt to excite the heart of God. I feared hurting myself—or at least, embarrassing myself—while dancing in those woods in Washington, but I knew it delighted God. Even history's great worship mentors sometimes struggled in their worship. Tozer said it well: "I cannot sing a lick, but that is nobody's business. God thinks I'm an opera star! I mean it when I say that I would rather worship God than do anything else on earth."[6]

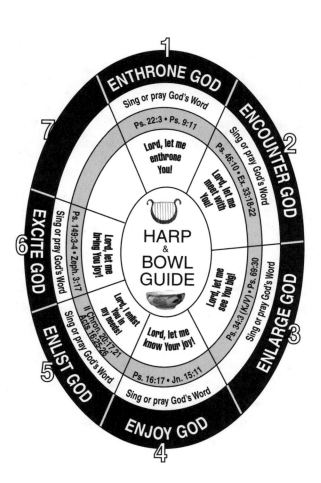

WORSHIP EXALTS GOD

CATCHING THE WAVE OF WORSHIP

"What on Earth is that?" my wife asked as she looked at a map of the world taped to the steering wheel of our car. It was December 1975.

"It's a map of the world," I answered—as if she couldn't tell what it was from two feet away.

"I can see that," she added, "but why on Earth would you tape it to the steering wheel?"

So began my daily prayer journey to the nations that has continued joyously for more than a quarter century. It is a deeply personal journey that I have been reluctant to describe in print, though it seems appropriate here as it relates so clearly to our final worship reality. (More about this unusual daily journey in a moment!)

All that has been discussed in the previous chapters, I believe, can be summed up in this final worship reality: *Worship exalts God!* In exalting God through worship we not only *enthrone* Him and *encounter* Him, but we *enlarge*, *enjoy*, *enlist* and *excite* Him.

All of this results in exalting God, which is at the heart of all true worship and leads to the releasing of the ultimate fulfillment of God's plan for humankind. That plan, I am convinced, is the completion of Christ's Bride and all the earth being filled with God's transforming glory (see Isa. 11:9; Hab. 2:14).

FURNACE-ROOM ENCOUNTERS

The psalmist lays this important foundation for worship reality seven: "I will praise you, O Lord, among the nations; I will sing of you among the peoples . . . Be exalted, O God, above the heavens; let your glory be over all the earth" (Ps. 57:9,11). As alluded to in the previous chapter, we find many similar expressions throughout the psalms where praise is pictured as impacting all the nations. In this particular admonition these words stand out: "Let your glory be over all the earth."

Said succinctly as our final intercessory worship principle:

> *Worship provides the platform and power necessary to exalt God in the nations.*

John Piper again provides insight for this reality: "Worship . . . is the fuel and goal in missions. It's the goal of missions because in missions we simply aim to bring the nations into the white-hot enjoyment of God's glory. The goal of missions is the gladness of the peoples in the greatness of God. Missions begins and ends in worship."[1]

Piper concludes, "Missions is not the ultimate goal of the church. Worship is. Missions exists because worship does not. The Great Commission is first to delight yourself in the Lord (Ps. 37:4) and then to declare 'Let the nations be glad and sing for joy'" (Ps. 67:4).[2]

And that brings me back to the map on the steering wheel.

Very early in my ministry I began sensing a special burden for the nations of the world that grew out of prolonged seasons of just seeking God for the sake of seeking God. The church where Dee and I served as youth leaders in southern Wisconsin, long before the map experience, had a furnace room that I quickly commandeered for prayer because it was a warm place to sit alone during our freezing Wisconsin winters. Interestingly, it also was the coolest place to pray in Wisconsin's steamy summers.

I would retreat to this furnace room for longer times of prayer when I felt I needed to be alone and unhindered. And it was also there that a burden for the lost and for the nations of the world slowly began to saturate my praying.

A particularly powerful passage of God's Word that significantly impacted those early years was the psalmist's declaration of intercessory worship in Psalm 67. We read:

> May God be gracious to us and bless us and make his face shine upon us, that your ways may be known on earth, your salvation among all nations. . . . May the peoples praise you, O God; may all the peoples praise you. . . . God will bless

us, and all the ends of the earth will fear him (Ps. 67:1-3,7).

The Living Bible paraphrases that last verse: "Peoples from remotest lands will worship him," a thought that would ultimately become my lifelong obsession and so became a personal "life passage" of Scripture.

JACK'S MAP

The morning that I taped the map to my steering wheel, Dee and I and our two young daughters, Dena and Ginger (at the time just six and three), were preparing to visit Dee's sister and brother-in-law in Portland, Oregon, over the Christmas holidays. Six months earlier I had met Jack McAlister, the founder and president of Every Home for Christ, then known as World Literature Crusade.

Jack was pretty much responsible for the whole map episode. He had added significant fuel to the fire of my heart for the nations. At the time I had no idea that a year later I would join Jack and his organization as their director of prayer mobilization and then 12 years after that become their international president.

For years Jack had annually produced what he called the World Prayer Map, a simple map of the world that could be folded up and placed in one's Bible. Jack's map listed all the 210 nations of that time in various strategic categories (e.g., all the communist nations in a group, all the Arab-Muslim nations together, etc.).

In that first meeting with Jack in May of 1975, he handed me one of these maps and rather pointedly asked me how many nations of the world I prayed for daily. I told him two—China and America, which was stretching the truth, because I probably prayed for China every third day.

> Quite possibly, it was the most significant prayer challenge of my entire life.

My prayers up to that time were much more general— for souls and missionaries. And even then, they were not very specific. I prayed many "bless 'em" prayers: bless the lost, bless the missionaries and bless all the churches in the whole wide world! Jack did not seem impressed.

Not one to skirt issues, Jack quickly added, "Maybe that's why so little is happening in so much of the world! You're only praying for two nations out of 210."

This unique leader, whom I had only met about 30

minutes earlier concluded, "You know, Dick, God answers specific prayers because praying specifically requires faith. Here, take this map. Maybe it will help you pray more specifically."

I had never met someone quite so blunt, but that encounter changed my prayer life. Quite possibly, it was the most significant prayer challenge of my entire life.

Conviction settled that day, and I determined I would pray for many more countries in the future. Because a systematic plan always helps me remain faithful, I decided to pray for one group of 30 countries each day. I divided the 210 countries by seven, one group for each day of the week, and marked off these listings on the map accordingly. I counted 30 nations and drew a line in ink, then counted another 30, and so on. This all began in the early summer of 1975.

But about midway through that following December, as I prayed over my 30 countries for a particular day, an overwhelming concern for the other 180 nations I had not prayed for came over me.

Tears came as I held the map in my hands, praying. I proceeded to pray for all the remaining nations on the map and then clutched the map silently for a few moments. Quietly I prayed, "God, if you'll just give me the strength and desire, I'll try to make this a daily habit for the rest of my life."

I knew it was a challenging commitment, but I felt I had to try.

Next, I decided to commit these countries to memory to help my prayer be more than merely reading a list, and I felt that a good time to do this would be during the drive from Sacramento to Portland, and back, over the holidays. I knew that I could look down periodically at the map and memorize the countries during the trip. By the time we returned from out trip to Portland, I had committed all 210 countries to memory. Thus, the map taped to the steering wheel!

A JOURNEY TO THE NATIONS

So began my daily journey of prayer to the nations that has continued for more than 25 years. Little could I have known how Jack's challenge and this world focus would impact my life and ministry. When I first memorized these nations, I did not memorize them in alphabetical order, but rather, memorized them according to Jack's geographical and political listings.

For example, Jack grouped all the communist nations

in one list for special prayer. He did the same for all the Arab-Muslim nations. Then, all the islands and smaller nations with populations less than a million each appeared on a separate list. These listings were added to the map itself that showed all the continents and locations of nations, together with numbers to correspond to his various lists.

Jack had begun Every Home for Christ in 1946. Interestingly, when I began praying for all these nations, I was not even working for the EHC ministry. Seventeen years after memorizing these nations from Jack's map, I was the international president of EHC and still praying daily for the nations.

So here I was in my prayer closet in Colorado, in February of 1992, praying once again for all the nations, in the order that I had memorized them back in 1975. As I came to my mental list of the communist lands, I began to pray for each by name. Tears unexpectedly began to flow as I was overwhelmed with a sudden realization of the power of simply exalting God over the nations, day by day, year after year.

You see, when I had begun that daily discipline some 17 years earlier, none of the communist lands was open to any free expressions of evangelism. Home-to-home evangelism of a systematic nature, such as Every Home for Christ conducts, was strictly forbidden in each of them. What little evangelism were happening in those nations was highly clandestine. Now, all but one were open—North Korea—and signs indicate this nation might not be closed to the gospel for very long.

Not only were most of these nations now open to the gospel, but Every Home for Christ was actually working directly in all of these nations but two—Laos and North Korea. By 1992 the Berlin Wall had come crashing down and all of Eastern Europe was open to the gospel. And by this time more than 2 million households in less than a year had already been reached by Every Home for Christ, just in the former Soviet Union!

A few days before this 1992 prayer encounter, word had reached our headquarters in Colorado Springs that an every-home initiative had been officially approved in the once highly restricted communist nation of Albania.

We were especially amazed to hear that Albania's new president had actually invited our EHC coordinator for Albania to his home and personally served him afternoon tea. The president also gave him his personal blessing to launch an effort to take the printed gospel message to every home in Albania (eventually touching some 800,000 homes where 3.5 million Albanians live).

Seventeen years earlier, when my daily prayers for Albania had begun, it was a nation in which it had been a capital crime to be a Christian or even possess a Bible.

Frankly, when I first began praying for all these nations, I could not have imagined anything like this happening in my lifetime. Now, it was not only happening, but also our own ministry was privileged to be directly involved in sharing the gospel, systematically, home to home, in all but two of these nations. And in some of these nations the results have been profound. As mentioned in chapter 3, over 40 million households in the former Soviet Union and Eastern Bloc countries already have been reached with a printed gospel message in the various languages of the region. Who could have imagined this even two decades ago?

Over the years since that 1992 encounter, considerably more has happened in this regard, including the emergence of a campaign in China that already has touched some 35 million Chinese households in just 36 months. Even more recently, a comprehensive plan has emerged that seeks to mobilize and train Chinese house-church networks, with as many as 3 million believers in a single network. Church leaders have agreed to take a printed gospel presentation to all 335 million Chinese households over a five- to seven-year period.

Additionally, outside teams of trained Westerners, as part of a well-organized plan, have blanketed hundreds of urban and rural areas with the gospel throughout China. As I described in my book *Beyond Imagination*, I joined one of these early teams in 1995 and saw firsthand many answers to my personal ongoing prayers. At the time I joined that team, 50 or 60 Chinese cities had been visited by these teams. Now the number is a staggering 900!

FORTY DAYS OF DELIGHT

But something very special, and unique, was about to happen regarding my daily journey of prayer to the nations. And it happened as my 40-day worship fast began in March of 2000 (see chapter 1).

You will recall that God impressed on my heart that I was to spend my times of daily prayer, for 40 days, entirely in worship. I was to sing all my prayers. But this posed for me an interesting dilemma. For 25 years I had prayed daily for all the nations, in addition to my usual focuses of prayer. Now it seemed God was leading me to worship Him purely in song during my times of prayer.

"Lord," I asked, during the first day of my worship fast, "are you asking me to suspend my usual daily prayers for the nations for the next 40 days?"

The Lord responded with His own question: *Did not My servant David sing among the nations?*

Immediately, I recalled that passage in the psalms where King David declared, "I will thank you, Lord, in front of all the people. I will sing your praises among the nations" (Ps. 57:9, *NLT*).

The Lord then spoke again: *Instead of praying for the nations each day during these coming 40 days, I want you to sing over the nations, daily, declaring My glory in song among all these peoples.*

And so it was that forty days of delightful intercessory worship followed. Each day my song was different, as I exalted God by singing over the 237 nations that Every Home for Christ now has listed on its updated World Prayer Map.[3]

It seemed fitting that, as the fast concluded on Palm Sunday, Dee and I headed to Hong Kong for our first-ever Harp and Bowl conference, which was scheduled to be held over the Easter holiday (a national holiday in Hong Kong).

During those days, prolonged times of worship and intercession ensued, with daily sessions of continuous, spontaneous intercessory worship lasting for two and three hours. More than two-thirds of the participants were from traditional, mainline denominational churches and were *not* generally accustomed to such free-flowing worship. Yet, they all entered in.

Neither my wife nor I could ever recall witnessing so deep a desire for God manifested in such sustained worship. The sounds were truly heavenly and at times I felt like I, too, heard supernatural songs. I also knew this worship would impact the nations, especially nearby China, because worship is not only the ultimate goal of missions, as John Piper suggests, but it is also the power propelling us toward that goal.

The impact of our prayer proved to be a reality in what happened in our ministry, particularly in China, in the weeks immediately following the exalting and enthroning of God so intensely in Hong Kong. It was, in fact, by that following September, just five months later, that the plan I mentioned earlier to reach every home in China really fell into place. I believe the sustained worship in Hong Kong helped release that plan, which is now well underway in spite of many obstacles.

PRESENCE EVANGELISM

Intercessory worship, indeed, is central to the accelerated harvest taking place throughout the world today.

I agree with Mike Bickle, who wrote in *Pray!* magazine:

> The Holy Spirit is orchestrating a global strategy far eclipsing any other prayer movement in history. This movement will be comprised of many diverse models and streams within the Body of Christ. This many-faceted prayer movement will result in an unprecedented harvest of souls and the completing of the Great Commission. It will become common to hear "intercessory worship" ministries that continue non-stop 24 hours a day.[4]

Already this continuous intercessory worship movement is spreading, emerging in such places as Kansas City; Colorado Springs; Washington, D.C.; Tel Aviv; Jerusalem; and even now in Hong Kong—all of which are well on their way to becoming sustained, 24-hour ministries of intercessory worship. Interestingly, in all of these places a wide range of streams from throughout Christ's Body are involved. You, too, can join this movement daily:

*Declare in song and prayer that
God is exalted over every need, opportunity
and nation on Earth.*

The suggestion that sustained worship around God's throne creates a throne zone where we can bring heaven to Earth through intensified worship is becoming a reality. I believe it is the result of this intercessory worship movement.

Tommy Tenney believes such worship will lead to what he calls presence evangelism, which he describes as a manifestation of God's presence in a region or city that is so overwhelming that unsaved people are drawn simply by a deep, inexplicable desire to seek and find the Lord.

Tenney illustrates this in his book *God's Favorite House* with an account that occurred in Georgia. The manifest presence of God began to impact a congregation and spill over into the community.

One Sunday an unchurched woman, half a mile away from the church where the congregation met, sat in her living room watching television. She later testified that she was drinking a Bud Lite, smoking a cigarette and channel surfing on her television when the unmistakable presence of God filled her living room. Fearing this strange presence rather than welcoming it, the woman ran into the kitchen.

Tenney explains that for a full week the woman refused to go into the living room because of this unusual presence.

But then, suddenly, this presence came into her kitchen. So for days she stayed in her bedroom.

That Sunday the woman showed up at the very church that had been experiencing God's presence in such unusual ways. There she told of her experience. She related, "This morning when I got up, it [the unusual presence] had pushed all the way into my bedroom and I could not run anymore! I knew it was coming from here, I just had to come."[5]

Tenney explains that the woman gave her heart to Jesus that night, illustrating how he believes presence evangelism can invade a city. The author concludes, "If you take this woman's testimony and multiply it by hundreds, thousands, and millions of lives, you might have a glimpse of what God has in store for this generation if we can create a throne zone of His presence."[6]

A SHOCKWAVE OF PRAISE

Could it be that this growing stream of intercessory worship—the harp and bowl (see Rev. 5:8) is directly linked to the ultimate fulfillment of the prophecy of Amos? (Amos 9:11-12; Acts 15:16-18).

It is here we read of David's fallen tent, or kingdom, being someday restored "so that the rest of humanity might find the Lord, including the Gentiles" (Acts 15:17, *NLT*).

David's tent is clearly a reference to the Tabernacle that David first set up in Jerusalem when he moved the Ark of the Covenant from its captivity in Gibeon. It was during this move that "David danced before the LORD with all his might" (2 Sam. 6:14, *NLT*) and instituted what ultimately would become continuous praise and worship—something we have been referring to as intercessory worship.

I believe that this prophetic declaration in Acts 15:17 (*NLT*) that "the rest of humanity" will "find the Lord, including the Gentiles" hinges on the restoration of a spirit of intercessory worship unlike anything the world has ever experienced. I am convinced that only a restoration of a passion for God's presence will transform whole nations.

So vital is this subject that my second book in this trilogy on intercessory worship, *Patterns of Delight*, deals exclusively with this theme: how restoring the tabernacle of David affects the destiny of nations. It is there that I share the spiritual "design" of David's Tabernacle and how its restoration—not as a structure but as an intercessory worship movement—will lead to what I am convinced will be the total transformation of entire communities, peoples and eventually whole nations through the gospel of Jesus Christ.

Here I will simply suggest that something remarkable has already begun, and it is obviously exciting. It is a wave of intercessory worship that is swelling and rising, ready to break into a sweeping, global release of the glory of God. Pastor Rick Warren of Southern California's thriving Saddleback Church often says in his seminars, "When you see a wave, catch it and ride it."[7]

Joseph Garlington, one our nation's gifted worship leaders and a prominent Promise Keeper speaker, adds this provocative observation: "One of the things under-girding the expansion of the kingdom of God is a new concept of praise. Something mighty is taking place in the earth. Praise and worship are at the center of what is happening. The shock wave of our praise is unaffected by distance, different time zones, or different languages, cultures, and political systems. It is a spiritual force to be reckoned with, and the church is just now catching on to this truth."[8]

Intercessory worship is, indeed, a wave—and a big one at that. It is rising as you read this. Let's catch it and ride it so that the world will never be the same.

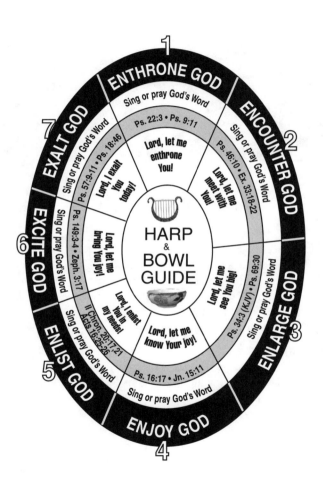

ENDNOTES

Introduction

1. For information on obtaining two unique "live" CDs recorded at the World Prayer Center (by worship leader Terry MacAlmon) write: Terry MacAlmon Ministries, P.O. Box 62501, Colorado Springs, CO 80962.
   Web site: www.terrymacalmon.com

Chapter One

1. Ed Reese, *The Life and Ministry of David Livingstone* (Glenwood, IL: Fundamental Publishers, 1975), p. 5.
2. I do not believe this vision encounter suggests that every person in every village and home on earth will someday be saved. However, I take great encouragement from such passages of Scripture as Isaiah 11:9 and Habakkuk 2:14 that prophesy the earth will be "filled" with the knowledge and glory of the Lord "as the waters cover the sea." The New

Living Translation of Isaiah 11:9 is especially inspiring: "as the waters fill the sea, so the earth will be filled with people who know the Lord."

3. Don Melvin, "Under African Skies," *Minneapolis Star Tribune,* January 15, 2000, p. B5.

4. *Transformations* videos (I and II) available from The Sentinel Group, P.O. Box 6334, Lynnwood, WA 98036.

5. "Intercessory worship" is an expression that I first heard through the ministry of Mike Bickle.

6. John Piper, *Let the Nations Be Glad* (Grand Rapids, MI: Baker Book House, 1993), p. 11.

7. Jack W. Hayford, *Worship His Majesty* (Waco, TX: Word Books, 1987), p. 191.

8. A. W. Tozer, *That Incredible Christian* (Camp Hill, PA: Christian Publications, 1964), p. 46.

9. A. W. Tozer, *Whatever Happened to Worship?* (Camp Hill, PA: Christian Publications, 1985), p. 56.

10. Ibid., p. 86.

11. The three books in the author's Delight Trilogy include this book, *Heights of Delight,* and two forthcoming books titled *Patterns of Delight,* and *Rivers of Delight.*

Chapter Two

1. Joseph Garlington, *Worship: The Pattern of Things in Heaven* (Shippensburg, PA: Destiny Image Publishers, Inc., 1997), p. 1.

2. Jack W. Hayford, *Worship His Majesty* (Ventura, CA: Regal Books, 2000), p. 158.

3. Every Home for Christ (formerly World Literature Crusade), is a worldwide ministry of house-to-house evangelism that has

been working actively since 1946 with more than 500 mission agencies and denominations to place a printed message of the gospel (one for adults and one for children) in every home in the whole world. Since its inception, EHC, with a full-time staff of over 1,200 workers plus over 2,400 volunteer associates, has distributed over 1.9 billion gospel messages, resulting in over 26 million decision cards being mailed to EHC's many offices overseas and the establishing of 39,000 village New Testament fellowships called "Christ Groups." Where illiterate people-groups exist, EHC distributes gospel records and audiotapes. In a recent 12-month period 1,485,284 decision cards were received in EHC offices around the world, or an average of 4,069 every day. Because many areas of the world are virtually closed to Christian outreach, particularly in Middle Eastern countries, Every Home for Christ has developed an especially strong prayer mobilization effort through its multi-hour Change the World School of Prayer, originated by Dick Eastman. More than 2,000,000 Christians in 120 nations have been impacted by this training.

4. Tommy Tenney, *God's Favorite House* (Shippensburg, PA: Destiny Image Publishers, Inc., 1999), pp. 66-67.

5. A quote from George Barna's research given in a cassette teaching by Robert Stearns, *The Tabernacle of David* (tape #2), Kairos Publications, Kairos, NY.

6. Tenney, p. 122.

Chapter Three

1. A. W. Tozer, *Whatever Happened to Worship?* (Camp Hill, PA: Christian Publications, 1985), p. 62.

2. Ibid., p. 88.
3. Ibid., p. 31.
4. Ibid., p. 30.
5. A. W. Tozer, *The Quotable Tozer I* (Camp Hill, PA: Christian Publications, 1984), p. 89.
6. Ibid., p. 99.
7. For an introductory CD Rom of Every Home for Christ's *Complete the Commission Strategic Plan*, write: EHC, P.O. Box 35930, Colorado Springs, CO 80935; or e-mail to: info@ehc.org.
8. Francis of Assisi, *The Writings of Francis of Assisi*, trans. Benen Fahy, O.F.M. (Chicago: Franciscan Herald Press, 1976), p. 8.
9. A quote often attributed to Francis of Assisi. Although the source is unknown, the sentiment is well within the spirit of the way Francis of Assisi conducted his life.

Chapter Four

1. John Piper, *Let the Nations Be Glad* (Grand Rapids, MI: Baker Book House, 1993), p. 40.
2. A. W. Tozer, *The Quotable Tozer II,* comp. Harry Verploegh (Camp Hill, PA: Christian Publications, 1997), p. 202.
3. A. W. Tozer, *Whatever Happened to Worship?* (Camp Hill, PA: Christian Publications, 1985), p. 44.
4. Joseph Garlington, *Worship: The Pattern of Things in Heaven* (Shippensburg, PA: Destiny Image Publishers, Inc., 1997), p. 109.
5. Max Lucado, *Just Like Jesus* (Dallas: Word Publishing), pp. 77-79.
6. Ibid., p. 82.

7. Bruce Watson, "Science Makes a Better Lighthouse Lens," *Smithsonian,* (August 1999) n.p.

Chapter Five

1. Gordon Morse, *My Molokai* (Volcano, HI: Island Publishing, 1990), p. 17.
2. Madame Guyon, *An Autobiography* (Chicago: Moody Press), p. 67.
3. Ibid., p. 94.
4. Francis of Assisi, *The Writings of Francis of Assisi*, trans. Benen Fahy, O.F.M. (Chicago: Franciscan Herald Press, 1976), p. 52.
5. Ibid., p. 52.
6. Brother Lawrence, *The Practice of the Presence of God* (Old Tappan, NJ: Spire Books, Fleming H. Revell Co., 1958), p. 45.
7. A.W. Tozer, *Whatever Happened to Worship?* (Camp Hill, PA: Christian Publications, 1985), p. 30.
8. Mike Bickle, *Pray!* (July/August 2000), p. 19.
9. Ibid., p. 19.
10. Ibid., p. 18.

Chapter Six

1. A.W. Tozer, *Whatever Happened to Worship?* (Grand Rapids, MI: Baker Book House, 1985), p. 18.
2. Ibid., p. 86.
3. Tommy Tenney, *God's Favorite House* (Shippensburg, PA: Destiny Image Publishers, Inc., 1999), p. 72.
4. Ibid., p. 72.

5. Ibid., p. 71.

6. *International Herald Tribune*, April 23, 1998, p. 4.

7. Dextel Filkins of the *LA Times*, quoted in the *Denver Post*, February 15, 1999, section A, p. 14.

8. Ibid., emphasis added.

Chapter Seven

1. A.W. Tozer, *Whatever Happened To Worship?* (Camp Hill, PA: Christian Publications, 1985), p. 61.

2. John Piper, *Let the Nations be Glad* (Grand Rapids, MI: Baker Book House, 1993), p. 15.

3. Ibid., p. 16.

4. Ibid., p. 21.

5. Ibid., p. 12.

6. Tozer, p. 18.

Chapter Eight

1. John Piper, *Let the Nations Be Glad* (Grand Rapids, MI: Baker Book House, 1993), p. 11.

2. Ibid., p. 40.

3. A copy of the most recent edition of the World Prayer Map can be ordered by calling Every Home for Christ, 1-800-423-5054; or write: Every Home for Christ, P.O. Box 35930, Colorado Springs, CO 80935; or visit EHC's website: www.ehc.org.

4. Mike Bickle, *Pray!* no. 19 (July/August 2000), p. 21.

5. Tommy Tenney, *God's Favorite House* (Shippensburg, PA: Destiny Image Publishers, Inc., 1999), p. 132.

6. Ibid., p. 132.

7. Rick Warren, pastors conference, August 8, 1997, Assemblies of God General Council, St. Louis, MO.

8. Joseph Garlington, *Worship: The Pattern of Things in Heaven* (Shippensburg, PA: Destiny Image Publishers, Inc., 1997), p. 129.

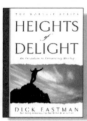
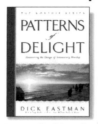
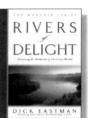

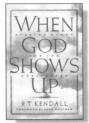
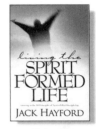

Every Home for Christ . . .
Reaching the Nations One Family at a Time!

Every Home for Christ, led by Dr. Dick Eastman, author of *Heights of Delight,* is a global home-to-home evangelism ministry (formerly known as World Literature Crusade) that has worked with more than 500 denominations and mission organizations to conduct Every Home Campaigns in 190 nations.

Since its inception, Every Home for Christ, with a full-time staff of over 1,200 workers plus over 2,400 volunteer associates, has distributed over 2.1 billion gospel messages home by home, resulting in over 27.5 million decision cards being mailed to EHC's numerous offices overseas and the establishing of over 43,000 village New Testament fellowships called "Christ Groups." Where illiterate people groups exist, EHC distributes gospel records and audiotapes, including the amazing "card talks" (cardboard record players). In one recent 12-month period 1,485,284 decision cards were received in EHC offices around the world, or an average of 4,069 *every day!*

To date, Every Home Campaigns have been conducted in 190 countries and completed in 90. The EHC ministry presently maintains 100 offices throughout the world, including much of the former Soviet Union and all 32 provinces and autonomous regions of China.

Because some areas of the world are virtually closed to Christian outreach, particularly in Middle Eastern countries, Every Home for Christ has developed an especially strong prayer mobilization effort through its multi-hour *Change the World School of Prayer* originated by Dick Eastman. More than 2,000,000 Christians in 120 nations have been impacted by this training, portions of which are now on DVD (video) in over 50 languages.

EHC's *Feed 5000* campaign enables believers to reach at least 5,000 people with the Gospel, over the course of a year. *Feed 5000* gives individuals a way to put feet to their prayers for the lost by providing gospel booklets and Bible-study materials that present Jesus, "the Bread of Life," for families who need to discover His offer of salvation.

Dick Eastman invites you to learn more about this opportunity by contacting Every Home for Christ for a full-color Lighthouse Edition of EHC's World Prayer Map along with information about how to become involved in feeding 5,000 the Bread of Life annually.

In the USA: Call toll-free 1-800-423-5054
Also, in the USA: 1-719-260-8888
P.O. Box 35930, Colorado Springs, CO 80935
In Canada: 1-800-265-7326
450 Speedvale Ave #101, Guelph, Ontario N1H 7X6
For other global addresses, contact EHC in the USA.
Visit our website at www.ehc.org